Myths of Free Trade

Myths of Free Trade

Why American Trade Policy Has Failed

Sherrod Brown

THE NEW PRESS

NEW YORK
LONDON

Requests for permission to reproduce selections from this book should be mailed to:
Permissions Department, The New Press, 38 Greene Street, New York, NY 10013.

First paperback edition published in the United States by The New Press, New York, 2006
Distributed by W. W. Norton & Company, Inc., New York

LIBRARY OF CONGRESS CATALOGING-IN-PUBLICATION DATA
Brown, Sherrod, 1952–
Myths of free trade: why American trade policy has failed / Sherrod Brown.
p. cm.
Includes index.
ISBN-13: 978-1-56584-928-0 (hc.) 978-1-59558-124-2 (pbk.)
ISBN-10: 1-56584-928-0 (hc.) 978-1-59558-124-3 (pbk.)
1. United States—Commercial policy.   2. Free trade—United States.
3. Social justice—United States.   I. Title.

HF1455.B733 2004
382'.71'0973—dc22   2004042619

The New Press was established in 1990 as a not-for-profit alternative to the large,
commercial publishing houses currently dominating the book publishing industry.
The New Press operates in the public interest rather than for private gain, and is
committed to publishing, in innovative ways, works of educational, cultural,
and community value that are often deemed insufficiently profitable.

www.thenewpress.com

Composition by dix!

Printed in the United States of America

2   4   6   8   10   9   7   5   3   1

To America's hourly wage earners who built a nation which is now letting them down.

And to those workers around the world who have yet to benefit from the fruits of their labor.

All author's proceeds from the sale of this book will go to RESULTS and Cleveland Jobs with Justice, two organizations committed to social and economic justice.

Contents

Acknowledgments

In the first edition I thanked many of those who care so deeply about globalization and who are, in the words of fair trader Theodore Roosevelt, "in the arena" and who are spending themselves "in a worthy cause." That list—with the passage of time and the challenge of CAFTA—has grown significantly.

Some new people have joined the fight: Joanna Kuebler, Brett Gibson, Jack Dover, and my entire office who were the primary reason the vote was so close. They worked long hours, never gave up, faced down huge odds, and made history.

The CAFTA coalition transcended political party and political ideology, building a movement—inside and outside the halls of Congress—which helped to swell public opposition to this flawed agreement: Thea Lee and Scott Paul of the AFL-CIO; Jess Peterson from Ranchers-Cattlemen Action Legal Fund (R-CALF); sugar advocates Ruthan Geib, Jack Roney, and Parks Shackelford; Kevin Kearns and William R. Hawkins from USBIC; Chris Slevin and of course Lori Wallach of Global Trade Watch; Yvette Pena Lopes from the Teamsters; Tom Buis of the National Farmers Union; Kathy Ozer of the National Family Farm Coalition; Stephanie Weinberg from Oxfam; Holly Hart, David McCall, and Garry Hubbard of the United Steelworkers of America; Larry Weiss of the Citizens Trade Campaign;

Margrete Strand Rangnes from the Sierra Club; Jessica Walker Beaumont of the American Friends Service Committee; and Tim Reif, Julie Herwig, Jennifer McCadney, and Jerry Hartz.

The following members of Congress spoke out, lobbied their colleagues, joined us at news conferences, sent out letters, spoke at rallies, and brought us closer than we have ever come in a trade vote: Thomas Allen, Joe Baca, Tammy Baldwin, Xavier Becerra, Benjamin Cardoza, Russ Carnahan, Joseph Crowley, Artur Davis, Peter DeFazio, Rosa DeLauro, John Dingell, Lloyd Doggett, Gene Green, Raul Grijalva, Stephanie Herseth, Steny Hoyer, Stephanie Tubbs-Jones, Walter Jones, Marcy Kaptur, Dennis Kucinich, Barbara Lee, Sander Levin, Betty McCollum, Charlie Melancon, Mike Michaud, George Miller, Butch Otter, Frank Pallone, Bill Pascrell, Nancy Pelosi, Collin Peterson, Earl Pomeroy, Charlie Rangel, Tim Ryan, Linda Sanchez, Bernie Sanders, Jan Schakowsky, Allyson Schwartz, Brad Sherman, Adam Smith, Hilda Solis, Pete Stark, Ted Strickland, Bart Stupak, Ellen Tauscher, and Maxine Waters. I have never been prouder to be a member of Congress and count them as friends and colleagues.

And of course, to Emily, Elizabeth, Caitlin, Andy, Mike, Stina, and Connie—who live their values, and never, ever quit.

Introduction: Mythmaking

Loyalty to petrified opinion never yet broke a chain or freed a human soul.

—*Mark Twain*

Trade gets more one-sided coverage from the nation's mainstream media than any other issue. All serious-minded people, the *Wall Street Journal* and the *New York Times* tell us, support free trade. It is hardly debatable. On one side, they assure us, are former presidents and secretaries of state, all the nation's major newspapers, distinguished business leaders, and virtually all of America's major economists. On the other are Patrick Buchanan, Ralph Nader, Ross Perot, organized labor "bosses," and a few extremist groups and individuals who are supposedly interested only in pushing their personal agendas. Outspoken congressional opponents of the North American Free Trade Agreement (NAFTA) and China Permanent Normal Trade Relations (PNTR) were labeled reactionaries, stooges of organized labor, and anti-intellectual Luddites standing in the way of progress. Yet, even in the face of unrelenting media and elite support for the received wisdom of unrestricted "free trade," the American public still has major reservations about United States trade policy.

Myths of Free Trade explains why the public is right and America's

elite are wrong. If the leaders of our institutions would take the time
to listen to people who work with their hands, they might learn something about the reasons for workers' anxiety, about the hopelessness
with which many look to the future, and about social justice. And
they would see that unregulated free trade hurts more people than it
helps—not only in the United States, but throughout the world.

The narrow passage by Congress of the North American Free
Trade Agreement in November 1993 masks the unevenness of the debate. The *Washington Post* gave pro-NAFTA arguments literally six
times the space in its editorials and op-ed pieces. The *New York Times*
quoted three NAFTA supporters for every one opponent in its news
coverage. When Democratic Whip David Bonior of Michigan wrote a
piece about NAFTA, the *Washington Post* censored the part of it that
was critical of the paper's coverage of the issue.

Most tellingly, a few days before the vote in the House of Representatives, Common Cause, the self-styled "good-government"
group, unveiled a study detailing the contributions from organized
labor that anti-NAFTA members of Congress had received. Common
Cause president Fred Wertheimer declined, when asked, to do a similar report on contributions to NAFTA supporters. "The elites of
media, business, academia, and politics," wrote journalist William
Greider, "have already made up their minds on these questions. They
are committed to promoting the global economic system—and to defending it from occasional attacks from angry, injured citizens."

Eighteenth-century British economist Adam Smith, considered
the intellectual father of free trade, albeit without the certainty and
intolerance of his present-day disciples, wrote in his book *The Nature
and the Causes of the Wealth of Nations:*

> The member of parliament who supports every proposal for
> strengthening this monopoly [of manufacturers] is sure to

acquire not only the reputation of understanding trade, but great popularity and influence with an order of men whose members and wealth render them of great importance. If he opposes them, on the contrary, and still more if he has authority enough to be able to thwart them, neither the most acknowledged probity, nor the highest rank, nor the greatest public service, can protect him from the most infamous abuse and detraction, from personal insults, nor sometimes from real danger, arising from the insolent outrage of furious and disappointed monopolists.

Smith could have been describing the media in the late-twentieth century. With its free-trade fervor and its conservative bias on economic issues, the Washington press corps was overwhelmingly supportive of the North American Free Trade Agreement and of Fast Track, the legislation proposed by President Bill Clinton and the Republican leadership in Congress that would have given the president the authority to extend NAFTA to Latin America.*

---

*A media-watch group, Fairness and Accuracy in Reporting, surveyed the Washington press corps in the late 1990s on a wide range of economic issues. The 441 respondents—reporters and editors alike—were "to the right of the public" on almost every major point. The journalists were asked about the following issues: protecting Medicare and Social Security; implementing and expanding NAFTA; enacting stricter environmental laws; requiring employers to provide health insurance to their employees; reigning in concentrated corporate power; taxing the wealthy; implementing fast-track negotiating authority; and instituting government guaranteed medical care. Only on the environment were the journalists "to the left" of the general public. Given the statement, "Too much power is concentrated in the hands of a few large companies," 24 percent of journalists strongly agreed, while 62 percent of the public strongly agreed. Perhaps the media's conservative, probusiness bias should come as no surprise; the survey showed that two-thirds of media respondents were male, 89 percent were white, 95 percent were college graduates, and 95 percent had personal incomes over $50,000 (52 percent earned more than $100,000). Their support of

An unregulated global economy is a threat to all of us—to the child in Avon Lake, Ohio, who eats raspberries grown in Guatemala by poorly paid farmers who use pesticides banned in the United States; the unskilled, minimum-wage worker in Los Angeles who loses her job to an unskilled, five-dollar-a-day worker in Yucatan; the machinist in New York who takes a wage cut because of his company's threat to move to China; the Chinese prison camp laborer; the tomato grower in Florida who has to sell his farm; and the peasant in Chiapas who must flee the native village where his family had made its home for dozens of generations. But our national leaders—particularly Republican congressional leaders and Presidents Clinton and Bush, economists and newspaper editors, business executives and tenured economics professors—continue to ignore the uncomfortable consequences of free trade, hoping the American public will not take notice. For example, Americans overwhelmingly support minimum wage and worker safety laws, yet in the global economy our leaders negotiate trade agreements that ignore the needs of workers. Many in Congress have fought for years for clean air, food safety, and safe drinking water laws, yet when our nation's trade representatives sit down at the negotiating table, they forget the environmental advances that we as a nation have fought for.

Our political leaders support—and excuse—authoritarian leaders in China and Indonesia because our corporate leaders have identified these totalitarian societies as ideal places to invest and reap huge profits, almost always selling back into the U.S. market the goods that

---

free trade was completely at odds with the general public. Sixty-five percent of Washington journalists believed that NAFTA's impact has been positive for the United States, while only 8 percent thought it has had a negative impact. Only 32 percent of the public believed NAFTA's impact has been positive, while 42 percent thought its impact has been negative. In the late 1990s, the Washington media supported Fast Track, 71–10 percent. The public opposed it, 35–56 percent.

slave labor or underpaid workers produce. Big business has ignored or put aside Chinese human rights abuses, security threats, theft of intellectual property, and loss of American jobs.

It is nothing new for the United States to do business with authoritarian regimes. In the past, we've done so to fight Communism, to help our largest corporations pilfer natural resources and open markets, and, most recently, to fight the war on terrorism and take advantage of low-wage workers. Once again, we are slavishly following the orders of dictators in a march of folly for which we almost always pay a price.

Since World War II, trade policy in the United States has been determined by a handful of members of Congress, a few bureaucrats at the Departments of State and Commerce, and several prominent lobbyist/attorneys at Washington's and New York's most prestigious law firms. It is my hope that *Myths of Free Trade* will help to broaden the debate on trade to include the American public. In the end, the American people, when better informed about trade, will demand that their elected representatives establish a trade policy that embodies the same American values that have long been embedded in our domestic policy.

1

Myth 1: Americans Believe in Free Trade

What is called sound economics is very often what mirrors the needs of the respectably affluent.

—*John Kenneth Galbraith*

The consensus on trade has fractured.

Fast Track was pulled off the floor of the House of Representatives within minutes of imminent defeat in 1997. The Multilateral Agreement on Investment was derailed. A second Fast Track bill was defeated decisively in 1998. The Battle in Seattle woke up the country about trade in 1999. It took more than 100 million corporate dollars and an unprecedented lobbying campaign to push through Congress legislation providing Permanent Normal Trade Relations with China in 2000. Even in the midst of a war on terrorism, with the United States trade representative invoking September 11, President Bush could push Fast Track, now renamed Trade Promotion Authority, through the House in December 2001 by just one vote. In September 2003, seventy developing nations rejected the demands of the richest nations to continue market liberalization, causing the collapse of the Cancún talks of the World Trade Organization. And in 2005 the Central American Free Trade Agreement squeaked through the House in a middle-of-the-night vote.

The myth that the American people support unregulated free trade is increasingly difficult to sustain. Yet the myth lives on in the nation's editorial boards, corporate suites, and academic think tanks. It is more than academic orthodoxy, more than media bias. It's a story of relentless corporate lobbying—and compliant government servants. And it is a story of growing popular resistance to the corporate consensus—no matter the myth.

The post–World War II global framework began in earnest when the United States joined the international trade negotiations at Bretton Woods in July 1944. In this bucolic setting in rural New Hampshire, the World Bank, officially known as the International Bank for Reconstruction and Development (IBRD), and the International Monetary Fund (IMF) were created, and the groundwork was laid for the General Agreement on Tariffs and Trade (GATT).

Soon to be victorious in the war, and looking out over a devastated Europe, America occupied center stage in the world economy. And for most of our postwar history, our trade policy and our larger foreign policy goals went hand in hand; making the world safe for American business became part of winning the Cold War. The United States used trade policy as an instrument in containing and defeating Communism. Our opposition to Communism was in part founded on our nation's belief in free enterprise, free markets, and promotion of business interests. Our foreign policy objectives, such as rebuilding the economies of Japan and Western Europe, were also aimed in those directions. So was our trade policy.

That explains, in part, our abhorrence of Soviet-style bureaucratic Communism, and our promotion—by the government and large businesses—of market Stalinism in China. But in winning the Cold War and helping to open up the world economy for American corporate investment, we lost, in the words of historian Alfred Eckes, "critical commercial battles . . . unilaterally [opening] the American market without gaining commensurate advantages in foreign markets for the products of American workers and American factories." Many American automobile workers, for example—who lost their jobs because the American automakers adapted so slowly to the changing market, and because Japan practiced the most aggressive kind of salesmanship and protectionism—felt betrayed by their government and by the auto companies.

In the three or so decades after Bretton Woods, few members of Congress understood trade laws, or had much interest in them. The influence of Commerce Department officials, lobbyists representing large corporations or foreign businesses and governments, and members of the House Ways and Means Committee was huge. A Washington publisher printed a book called *Trade Warriors: An Inside Look at Trade Activists in Congress—and How to Reach Them* to assist free-trade lobbyists in reaching key members of Congress in the trade debate. Published in 1986, it listed only thirty senators and forty-five House members, along with their voting records, the companies in their districts and states, and commentary on their positions on trade. Few others in Congress had any interest in or knowledge of the enormously complex trade laws. And apparently, no other members of Congress mattered much to America's trade establishment.

It was easy, then, for the free traders. In 1979 the GATT Tokyo-round agreements passed the Senate 83–9 and the House 366–40. In 1985 the House of Representatives approved the Israel free-trade agreement 422–0. Three years later, the Senate passed the Canada trade agreement 90–4; the House voted 395–7.

When free traders needed to lobby Congress, they almost never lost. The House Ways and Means Committee, where trade legislation is heard and passed, has always been the most pro–free trade collection of congressmen and congresswomen on Capitol Hill. Under long-standing House rules, trade bills typically may not be amended on the floor of the House of Representatives; they must be voted up or down with no changes—the only major category of legislation that Congress decides in this way. In *Saving Free Trade* (1986) by Robert Lawrence and Robert Litan, senior fellows at the Brookings Institution, the authors spoke for much of the nation's free-trade elite when they wrote, "The bill to impose quotas on imported textiles illustrates the dangers of adjustment policy in congressional hands." This attitude, dominant among the Washington establishment, permeated almost all business and trade publications from the 1950s until the 1980s.

The rest of the media were not much interested; after all, America was on top of the economic world, and trade mattered little to most Americans. The agreements were drafted behind closed doors by Commerce and State Department officials, partners at Washington's and New York's most prominent law firms, and many of America's largest corporations and their lobbyists. Little public light shone on the participants or their product. But when the first waves of Japanese automobile exports started to hit American shores in the 1970s and 1980s, the consensus over free trade began to crumble, and congressional opposition to our trade policy began to form. The winds of change that had blown across the country in the 1970s and 1980s became a storm in Congress in the 1990s.

President Richard M. Nixon had been the first president granted fast-track trade negotiating authority, giving him the ability to draft a trade bill without consulting Congress and then force a quick up or down vote from Congress with no changes to the bill allowed. Except for a half-year expiration in the late 1980s, fast-track negotiating authority was available to the executive branch from January 1975 to May 1993. But in 1991, when George H.W. Bush asked Congress for fast-track authority to negotiate a trade agreement with Mexico and Canada, a pitched battle ensued. The extension of fast track passed 231–192. Two years later, there was a colossal, yearlong struggle between pro- and anti–free-trade factions to pass the North American Free Trade Agreement.

When I came to Congress in 1993, I encountered a process during the NAFTA debate that would be repeated with every trade vote that came down the pike: The White House predicted economic disaster if the pact was defeated. The United States Chamber of Commerce anticipated a trade war. Mainstream economists tut-tutted that the stock market would crash. The Speaker of the House warned that there would be a recession.

Many Americans were skeptical. The debate in 1993 over NAFTA engaged the public, especially labor union members and devotees of Ross Perot, more than any other trade issue had for decades. During the debate, Atlanta congressman John Lewis, a NAFTA opponent, told me, "We are going to win this because we have passion on our side; our people care so strongly about this issue." I thought of John Stuart Mill's pronouncement: "One person with a belief is equal to a force of 99 who have only interests." Then-congressman Bill Richardson, a New Mexico free-trade Democrat and supporter of NAFTA, lamented congressional recesses in the summer and fall of 1993: "Every time members of Congress go home, our side loses votes. The public is really upset about this trade agreement," he admitted to me as the NAFTA vote approached.

Still, corporate lobbyists were everywhere. They flew in from all over the country; an airport official told us that there were more corporate planes at Washington National than he had ever seen. Democratic leadership aide Steve Elmendorf informed me that he had never seen a bill that the elite of this country wanted so badly. Full-page advertisements paid for by Merrill Lynch and other financial services companies appeared in *Roll Call,* the privately owned congressional newspaper, extolling the economic growth benefits of NAFTA.

Corporate executives invited us to tour the plants in our districts and told us that "NAFTA means jobs" at home. They encouraged and persuaded their employees to write letters about the benefits of NAFTA. One day, before I visited a pro-NAFTA company in Ohio, an employee of that firm—asking not to be identified—called me and whispered, "We were told by management that we are not to talk to the congressman unless we are pro-NAFTA. The meaning was clear that our jobs might be in jeopardy otherwise."

A Southern congressman received a call on a Friday from the wife of an official at a Fortune 500 company. She said that in spite of the call that the congressman would receive from her husband on Monday, there were two anti-NAFTA votes in her house. Indeed, on Monday the company official called and, as his boss sat there listening, said that he was pro-NAFTA.

The grocery manufacturers' trade association sent us the biggest food basket I've ever seen. Attached was a note: "All of this was Made in America. Vote for NAFTA so we can export more of this to Mexico." We sent it to a homeless shelter, as did most other anti-NAFTA activists in the House. We also responded with a statement to the press that a Mexican *maquiladora* worker would have to work two or three weeks to be able to afford the basket's contents.

Nestle, Inc., one of the big gainers from NAFTA, sent us a large basket of their products: Quaker Oats, Nestle's Crunch ("It's CRUNCH Time for NAFTA"), and "Capitan" Crunch (notice the Spanish spelling, letting us know that Nestle could sell a lot of cereal in Mexico). The Mexican government spent $25 million to lobby our government as well, hiring many of Washington's most powerful lobbyists, Democrat and Republican alike, and paying them huge amounts of money. But it was not only the Mexican government.

The Central Intelligence Agency conducted a briefing, reminiscent of a scene from a spy thriller, in a dimly lit room in the Capitol Building, with six men in dark suits telling us (in their affected, preppy, establishment manner of speech) that defeat of "the NAHF-ta" had national security ramifications. They seemed unable, however, to answer any questions or offer any information about the dozens of unsolved murders of leading Mexican labor activists, journalists, or political figures. Many of us walked away more certain than ever about the corruption in the highest levels of the Mexican government.

In the end, we fell just short of stopping NAFTA. It passed the House 234–200 and the Senate 61–38.

The subsequent passage, in December 1994, of the Uruguay round of the GATT, which set up the World Trade Organization (WTO), saw more of the same. The GATT's new provisions were scheduled for a floor vote one month after the Republicans won control of the House of Representatives for the first time in forty years. Democrats were stunned and wanted to get the session over with. Having been reelected by a small margin only three weeks earlier, I pleaded with several senior Democrats to push the GATT vote into the next Congress, handing the responsibility to Republican leadership to round up the votes. It would, I suggested, gum up the works in January as they prepared to pass soon-to-be Speaker Newt Gingrich's Contract with America. It also would have given us more time to bring attention to the antidemocratic features of the WTO. But dispirited Democrats simply shrugged.

Besides, the lobbying effort for this "NAFTA on steroids" became even more frenetic—and slicker—than it had been for the original NAFTA. Business, under the umbrella group USA GATT NOW, spent millions and had clearly learned something from their near-defeat on NAFTA. They sent packets of GATT NOW baseball cards to our offices, showing as All-Stars Bill Clinton ("President Clinton hit a home run for America by concluding the GATT agreement"), George H.W. Bush ("President Bush oversaw four crucial years of GATT negotiations, and helped make GATT a home run for America"), and Ronald Reagan ("President Ronald Reagan threw the opening pitch for the Uruguay round trade talks in 1986, helping to ensure today's GATT agreement—a home run for America"), each with a picture of the president throwing out the first ball at a Major League baseball game. Other All-Stars were the four United States trade representatives during the GATT negotiations—Mickey Kantor, Carla Hills, Clayton Yeutter, and William Brock. Each state also had its own card, so one could see the benefit of exports for that state. The final admonishment on the USA GATT NOW playing cards was: "Don't be left out . . . there are 58 USA GATT NOW trading cards . . . collect 'em all!"

The GATT agreement passed, and those trading cards became collectors' items to young Hill staffers. But after 1994, the free-trade scorecard never looked as good for the White House, Speaker Gingrich, and America's largest businesses. The 1994 GATT was the last major trade bill that came easily for the White House. Just three years later, in the biggest setback for free traders in the last half century, legislation granting the president new fast-track authority was taken off the House calendar by a frustrated and angry Gingrich, who knew the legislation faced certain defeat. And the following year, only six weeks before the November 1998 elections, the House overwhelmingly defeated Fast Track, 243–180.

The reverberations from the NAFTA debate ultimately derailed Fast Track. The public and many of us in Congress saw Fast Track as a referendum on NAFTA, and an international imitation of Gingrich's

Contract with America. We thought NAFTA had failed miserably, and voters increasingly had an intuitive sense that these trade agreements had cost jobs, lowered living standards, and done little or nothing to help the poor in the developing world.

Other significant victories soon followed. The Caribbean Basin Initiative, which would have expanded NAFTA to several Caribbean island nations, was defeated twice. The Africa Trade bill (labeled by many of us as NAFTA-for-Africa because it had even fewer protections for worker rights and health and safety standards than the Mexico-Canada-U.S. agreement) was delayed, as was a WTO enforcement bill. The Multilateral Agreement on Investment (MAI) died before it got to its final stages of negotiations.

If you look closely at the MAI, it becomes clear why ordinary people have become more and more alarmed by these arcane agreements—and not just folks in America, but those in developing countries as well. The MAI, like all international trade agreements, was prejudiced toward capital—focusing on the rights of investors—and unconcerned about the rights of workers and the environment. Put forward by the European Union in 1995 in a document called "A Level Playing Field for Direct Investment," it proposed to radically alter the role of local and state governments in enacting laws for their citizens. Under the agreement, countries would have had to roll back laws or regulations—such as minority set-aside programs, tax breaks for businesses locating in impoverished areas, and the awarding of public works contracts to environmentally responsible firms—that were not in compliance with the MAI's financial and performance requirements. More important, the expropriation sections of the MAI allowed international bureaucrats to override any law or regulation that corporations contended might affect profits, a loophole larger than any trade agreement ever negotiated among nations. Don't all health and safety regulations, at least to some degree, cost the company some money? Don't all environmental standards and worker safety requirements affect profits? Don't food safety regulations shrink return on investment? Don't minimum-wage laws affect the bottom line?

Under the MAI, power would have shifted even more dramatically from governments to markets. The agreement would have allowed corporations, in a sense, to write the constitution of a world economy with no real democratic controls. Even though protection for business interests—repatriation of profits, intellectual property rights, patents—is all done in the name of "free trade," free traders label standards for labor rights, food safety, and the environment "protectionism."

Developing countries were particularly concerned about the MAI. India immediately opposed it and was later joined by other nations. Stella Mushiri, a trade research analyst at ZIMTRADE, a protrade development organization in Harare, Zimbabwe, lamented, "It means you actually give up your sovereignty on the control of foreign investors in your country. We all want foreign investment, but we need to protect and nurture our own local investors. If it's going to be a free-for-all on equal terms, I don't think we are going to have a chance to develop our own local resources in terms of investment."

That kind of concern saw its ultimate expression in Seattle, when more than 30,000 mostly middle-aged steelworkers, machinists, and Teamsters joined 20,000 college students, environmentalists, religious leaders, and human rights advocates in opposition to the World Trade Organization's version of globalization. They walked together through the streets of Seattle peacefully and passionately. Peaceful in their belief that direct, nonviolent action might indeed wake up the country to trade injustices. Passionate in their opposition to a World Trade Organization that operates in secret and fails to consider labor rights and environmental standards. As I spoke at rallies, marched with demonstrators, and got a whiff of tear gas, I knew that we were making history. As I met with trade ministers, other members of Congress, and U.S. trade officials inside the barricaded hotels, I knew that they did not understand that.

The few hundred demonstrators who turned violent and caught the media's most direct attention informed the public that something big—not really seen in this country in over two decades—was happening in Seattle, the home of huge export businesses like Microsoft and (at that time) Boeing, and the site of America's only workers' general strike in 1919. Many columnists, unable to understand why hundreds of thousands of workers and students protested globalization in Seattle and elsewhere, accused them of selling out the poor.

The critics missed the point. It was simply too difficult for these writers to accept the notion that many critics of globalization were looking not for material gain but for simple justice. Almost all the demonstrators—environmentalists, trade union members, students, food safety advocates—wanted a WTO that is more democratic, more transparent, and less beholden to the world's largest multinational corporations. They wanted a WTO that would raise living standards around the globe. They wanted, in the words of Greg Coleridge of the American Friends Service Committee in Akron, a seat at the table where now "only government heads and international corporate representatives meet to debate often secret agreements that transform public arenas into private corporate arenas."

Three important things happened in Seattle. First, the depth of passion and breadth of support for enforceable labor and environmental standards surprised the delegates inside the halls. Few finance ministers and trade officials knew the strong beliefs of the protestors and the millions of workers they represented, both in the United States and around the world. The delegates had arrived in Seattle expecting a much easier time of it. They expected some opposition, to be sure, but mostly from people on the fringe, not a huge, passionate outcry from middle-class, middle-aged workers. Then when President Clinton flew to Seattle and delivered a message that labor standards— enforced with sanctions against those countries that did not abide by International Labor Organization standards—should be included in the core agreements of the WTO, their surprise turned to shock . . . and anger. Shock that Clinton, too, was supportive—or at least said he was—of enforceable labor standards, anger that negotiations with the United States were going to be appreciably more difficult.

The second important effect of the Seattle protests was that the media were equally surprised by such passion and support for labor standards. Ferocious attacks by the free-trade-at-all-costs pundits— Charles Krauthammer, George Will, Thomas Friedman, who really do not believe in labor standards even in the United States—confirmed, by their shrillness, that a growing number of Americans were questioning the unregulated global commerce which was central to our trade policy. Even pro–free trade newspapers like the *New York Times* and the *Washington Post* were opining that labor rights should in fact be considered as part of our nation's trade agreements.

The third and most important impact of Seattle was the heightened interest among the public in U.S. trade policy. But despite that intense interest, and the opposition victories of the 1990s, free traders continue to hold sway over Washington. Why? Consider this story about fish and officialdom: In July 1997, salmon farmers in Maine and Washington State won a unanimous preliminary ruling from the United States International Trade Commission that Chile was "dumping" salmon on the U.S. market. Steve Fought, who worked on trade issues in my office, discovered while surfing the Web one night that the Chilean government had hired former senator Bob Dole to represent Chile against U.S. salmon farmers. Dole had served as chairman of the Senate Finance Committee, the panel with jurisdiction over trade. By 1997 he was a partner in the prominent Washington, D.C., law firm Verner, Liipfert, Bernhard, McPherson and Hand, though only nine months earlier he had asked those fishermen and women to make him their president. When we called the Chilean embassy to confirm Dole's hiring, they gleefully told us what a coup it was to land such a prominent American politician to represent them in a dispute against United States citizens before a U.S. government agency. But anyone representing a foreign government before the United States Congress or a U.S. government agency must register as a foreign agent, and Dole hadn't. After we alerted the media, Dole responded angrily that his firm was simply giving advice, and that it was not necessary for him to register as a foreign agent for the government of Chile. Several months later I was told that behind closed doors at a law firm meeting, Dole angrily demanded to know who "that Ohio congressman was" who had outed him.

Although Bob Dole moved more quickly than most from prominent government official to foreign agent, he is hardly the only one; he just happens to be probably the best-known American government official ever to make that jump. Between 1972 and 1990, half of the U.S. trade negotiators who left government became foreign agents; with them, they took their connections and their skills in negotiating trade agreements to other American and foreign negotiators and to U.S. government officials. They also peddled their knowledge of U.S. trade law, some of which they had actually written, with full understanding of its history, its loopholes, and its nuances. In the 1980s, nine of nineteen trade officials from the Commerce Department signed up as foreign agents. Japan hired seven of them. In the early 1990s after President Bush left office, many of his top officials hired themselves out to foreign interests. The revolving door spun again when President Clinton left office.

In *Agents of Influence,* the definitive work on foreign lobbying and its effects on U.S. trade policy, economist and 1996 Ross Perot running mate Pat Choate cited some comments made about U.S. trade policy and its formulation and implementation around the world: "Influence in Washington is just like in Indonesia. It's for sale," wrote the *Japan Economic Journal.* The *Economist* opined, "America has the most advanced influence-peddling industry in the world. Washington's culture of influence-for-hire is uniquely open to all buyers, foreign and domestic. . . . Its lawful ways of corrupting public policy remain unrivaled." And a Dutch writer, Karel van Wolferen, wrote, "A big part of the problem is that Americans can be bought so easily."

Choate wrote, "Japan is running an ongoing political campaign in America as if it were a third major political party. It is spending at least $100 million each year to hire hundreds of Washington, D.C., lobbyists, superlawyers, former high-ranking public officials, public relations specialists, political advisers—even former presidents. It is spending another $300 million each year to shape American public opinion through its nationwide local political network."

Those words were written fifteen years ago. Dozens of other countries have since adopted Japan's tactics as a model for how to buy influence at the highest levels of government in Washington. China has now displaced Japan as Washington's preeminent cash cow for trade lobbyists. For example, Henry Kissinger founded the American China Society and housed it in his lobbying/consulting firm, Kissinger Associates. (Former New Mexico congressman Bill Richardson joined forces with Kissinger in the summer of 2001, then left to run successfully for governor of New Mexico.) Kissinger does not work directly for the Chinese government; no Washington lobbyists are actually retained by the People's Republic of China (though a Cleveland law firm—Jones, Day, Reavis and Pogue—has done legal work for the Chinese government).

From 1979 to 1994, registered foreign agents—American citizens representing foreign concerns and lobbying the U.S. Congress or executive branch—increased eightfold! Since then the numbers have continued to grow, and it is not only foreign countries these lobbyists represent. Literally thousands of American attorneys, former government officials, former congressmen and senators, and others represent American corporations that are doing business abroad and foreign companies doing business in the United States and looking for special treatment from Congress.

In this supercharged world of foreign-bought and corporate-owned influence, ordinary Americans don't get much of a hearing. Consider the case of steel. Every country that wants to be a player in the world economy has its own steel industry. Many subsidize it. Most export to the United States as much as possible. November 1998 steel imports into the United States, for example, increased 72 percent over imports one year earlier. Total imports in November 1998 were 37 percent of U.S. steel consumption, the highest on record; historically it stood at about 20 percent. Total 1998 steel imports were almost one-third higher than those in 1997, which itself was a record-setting year. Andrew Sharkey III, American Iron and Steel Institute (AISI) president and CEO, declared that "the U.S. remains the World's Steel Dumping Ground."

Tens of thousands of steelworker jobs were in peril. Thousands marched on Washington throughout 1998 and 1999. At least a score of congressmen and congresswomen from steel districts spoke out and introduced legislation. Speakers at rallies in Ohio, Indiana, Illinois, West Virginia, Pennsylvania, and Alabama—America's preeminent steelmaking states—were demanding help.

Hardest hit may have been the Ohio Valley in eastern Ohio and northern West Virginia. Fear of the future, a sentiment all too well-known in this part of America, filled the air in the Ohio River towns of Steubenville, Ohio, and Weirton, West Virginia. Every recession and economic downturn that afflicted America in the last quarter-century hit the Ohio Valley especially hard. But this one seemed worse. Almost a quarter of Weirton Steel's 4,000 employees had been laid off by November 1998. While the rest of America was prospering (or at least that's what Ohio Valley residents saw on television, and that's what the president had told the nation), to these steelworkers, the future looked no better than the already bleak present.

Rich Littleton, one of the laid-off steelworkers, sat in the union hall in Weirton in 1999 and lamented to *Columbus Dispatch* reporter Ron Carter, "I'm 38 years old. How marketable am I? This used to be something you could count on. I always wanted to do the same thing my father did. It scares me that I might not be able to give to my family the same things this place gave to me."

In 1984 the community and the employees of Weirton Steel saved the plant when they put together an Employee Stock Owner-ship Plan (ESOP), cut the administrative fat at the factory, and in-vested in new equipment and state-of-the-art technology. Rich Littleton's father and both his grandfathers had worked in the mill. Littleton's wife also worked in the mill. Weirton Steel laid her off along with her husband. Their combined annual income had ap-proached $70,000; now they had no idea about their future. "You don't know from one moment to the next whether you're going to be able to put food on the table or pay the rent. . . . This is what we know. This is what we do." In early 2004 ISG bought a bankrupt Weirton Steel.

The steel crisis put U.S. steel executives in a difficult position. They excoriated the president and Secretary of the Treasury Robert Rubin for their refusal to address the impending loss of jobs in their industry. In early 1999, as the crisis deepened, steel executives fanned out to Capitol Hill offices, imploring members of Congress to help.

They asked for congressional pressure on the president, political pressure on the vice president, and legislative action from us. One prominent Republican steel executive from Ohio came to my office and said, "Tell your friend Al Gore that he needs us, that he needs Ohio to win the election next year, and that he better step up to the plate." Steel executives felt betrayed by a president who was now, in their minds, dead wrong on trade. Until the steel crisis, however, they thought the president was consistently right on trade—on NAFTA, on GATT, on trade with China, and on Fast Track. Ironically, a stubborn consistency from a free trade president now mystified them. And a business class consistently on the wrong side—and a political class that refused to fight for fair trade—cost thousands of steelworkers their livelihoods.

In 2001 the problem grew markedly worse. Nationally, more than two dozen steel companies had declared bankruptcy since the crisis began three years earlier. Close to 50,000 jobs were lost. In northeast Ohio three steel companies filed for bankruptcy, jeopardizing at least 12,000 jobs. LTV, the third-largest integrated steel company in the United States, shut its doors, throwing 3,000 people out of work. On March 31, 2002, 45,000 retirees lost their health benefits. Retirees also feared that part of their pensions would be jeopardized. Congressional reaction was swift, until Republican leadership stopped dead in its tracks any legislative action.

Vice presidential candidate Cheney had promised in Wheeling, West Virginia, in October 2000 that he and George W. Bush would not sit idly by as America's steel industry crumbled. As bankruptcies mounted during Bush's first year in office, and as more than one million industrial jobs were lost, the pressure on the administration to act built rapidly. Bush invoked Section 201 of the Trade Act of 1974— a mechanism to set the stage for an investigation of unfair trade practices that would allow the president to slap significant tariffs on illegal dumped steel. But despite the warnings of United Steelworkers president Leo Girard and the CEOs of America's steel companies, the president hesitated in the early days of 2002, delaying the decision on whether to implement the tariffs. LTV idled its mills, and as LTV workers lost jobs, incomes, pensions, and health benefits, LTV executives reaped a bonanza. In a harbinger of things to come—a sort of Enron conservatism in which executives enrich themselves as they and market forces destroy companies—LTV's top executives gave themselves bonuses of several million dollars. Finally, the president did place significant tariffs on imported steel, giving some breathing room to the beleaguered industry but less than the industry thought was needed. President Bush then allowed the tariff to expire.

There is little loyalty on the part of many corporations to the communities in which their executives live and the country that they call home. The late Robert Bartley, head cheerleader for free trade's chief cheering squad, the *Wall Street Journal,* said hopefully, "I think the nation-state is finished." Former Clinton Labor Secretary Robert Reich said more sympathetically, "Gone is the tight connection between the company, its community, even its country. Vanishing too are the paternalistic corporate heads who used to feel a sense of responsibility for their local community. Emerging in their place is the new global manager." A spokesman for Union Carbide intoned: "It is not proper for an international corporation to put the welfare of any country in which it does business above that of any other." Those somber statements, of course, do not stop them from petitioning Congress for special tax advantages as American companies, lobbying for government contracts, asking American regulators for special dispensation, playing to American patriotism in their advertising, or even declaring their loyalty to the Cleveland Indians baseball team when advertising in Cleveland.

President George W. Bush, always on the side of America's most powerful corporations, set the tone of his administration in 2001 when he quietly delayed, then reversed, a new policy that blocked government contracts for companies that had defrauded the government. Law and order, apparently, only goes so far with conservative politicians.

The new global captains of industry assure us that if they can operate without interference from national governments, they will provide the capital and jobs to create huge, vibrant middle classes in dozens of developing countries. They tell us repeatedly to get out of the way. Without the burden of environmental rules and labor standards, they can lift hundreds of millions of people out of poverty. These corporations, obviously powerful forces in the media (which they own) and government (which they seem to lease), have convinced their countries to adopt economic policies that, as billionaire financier and European Parliament member Sir James Goldsmith said, "makes you rich if you eliminate your national workforce and transfer production abroad, and which bankrupts you if you continue to employ your own people." Stanley Mihelick, executive vice president of Goodyear, commented, "Until we get real wages down much closer to those of the Brazils and Koreas, we cannot pass along productivity gains to wages and still be competitive." Former General Electric CEO Jack Welch found the best way to chase cheap labor was to "have every plant you own on a barge."

The economic titans will continue to play off government against government, further weakening environmental and food safety standards in both nations, sapping governments' ability to govern, and unraveling our own system of self-government. Interference by government—as the most sophisticated among the world's elite keep telling us—is inefficient, problematic, and simply unnatural. Unshackle business. Allow the corporate engines to create untold wealth. Let the natural market forces play without political interference. And politicians, they assure us, are surely not to be trusted. What the elite really mean is that democracy is not to be trusted. Lewis Lapham wrote of the modern global capitalists he met at the World Economic Forum in Davos, Switzerland, in the spring of 1998:

> Having achieved their success by virtue of their talent for organization, they defined the dilemma of postmodern capitalism as a problem in management rather than a question of politics. Politicians were by definition untrustworthy, belonging to one of only two familiar types—light-minded demagogues stirring up crowds, or "pesky legislators" constantly bothering people with demands for bribes. Markets might have their flaws, but government was worse. Political interference wrecked the free play of natural distribution, and government never knew how to manage anything—not roads, not dairy farms or gambling casinos or capital flows. All would be well, and civilization much improved, if only politics could be manufactured in the way that one manufactured railroad cars or tomato soup.

A belief in the conscience of the market, with no checks by government or an economic power like labor, will spell disaster for democracy. A market economy without restraint—with no environmental or food safety rules, with no labor rights, with no labor unions—will undermine democratic institutions as all power accrues to a corporate elite. "If labor has no role," AFL-CIO president John Sweeney told the largely unsympathetic crowd at the World Economic Forum in Davos, "democracy has no future."

2

Myth 2: Free-Trade Agreements Are Necessary to Fight the War on Terrorism

Sometimes, tragedy also presents opportunities for those who are alert.

—*United States Trade Representative Robert Zoellick, October 2001*

Six decades ago, millions of Americans reacted as one to the tragedy of December 7, 1941, when the Japanese attacked Pearl Harbor, Hawaii. A stunned nation listened to the reassuring words of its leader, President Franklin Delano Roosevelt, as he called on citizens to fight for democracy and rally around the war effort. In a display of bipartisanship earlier in his administration, he had appointed two prominent Republicans to help lead the war effort—Frank Knox as Secretary of the Navy, and Henry Stimson as Secretary of the War Department.

President Roosevelt talked of "shared sacrifice." And the country responded. Millions of men and women stepped forward to volun-

teer for the armed services. Hundreds of thousands of women went to
work in industrial plants to fuel the war machine. Taxes were raised
on the wealthiest citizens to fund the war effort. People bought war
bonds, set up victory gardens, organized scrap metal drives.

To twenty-first-century Americans, the gruesome terrorist attacks of September 11, 2001, on two American symbols—the World
Trade Center and the Pentagon—seemed much like the Japanese assault on Pearl Harbor: thousands of Americans died; the attack was vi-
cious and the damage unimaginable; it appeared to have been planned
for months. The response to both tragedies seemed similar. President
George W. Bush asked for support and unity from the American people in a global fight against terrorism. Americans rallied around him
and the war effort. Young men and women called their local enlist-
ment offices. Millions of Americans put up flags—at their homes, in
their workplaces, on their SUVs. Hundreds of thousands of Americans donated blood, many for the first time in their lives. Tens of thousands volunteered to help rescue efforts at the Pentagon, at Ground
Zero in New York City where the Trade Center buildings had stood,
and in their communities. Thousands of schoolchildren collected
pennies and nickels and dimes to send to the victims and their families. And Americans by the millions honored the hundreds who lost
their lives, especially police and firefighters, who, in rescue efforts at
the World Trade Center, committed great acts of heroism.

But this unity looked very different inside the Washington Belt-
way. The ruins from the September 11 attacks were still smoldering
when the wartime political profiteering began. Administration officials called on Congress to immediately pass the stalled, and generally
accepted as unworkable, national missile defense program, as if that
would have stopped or deterred the airplane attacks on our nation.
Less than forty-eight hours after the attack, claiming it necessary to
prevent the economy from crashing, Republican House Ways and

Means chairman Bill Thomas of California tried to railroad through Congress a major cut in the capital gains tax; fully 80 percent of the benefits would have gone to 2 percent of taxpayers—the 2 percent at the top of the economic ladder.

Within days, Congress, at the insistence of President Bush, gave the beleaguered airlines $5 billion—no strings attached—with no sacrifice required from executives, no assistance for their 100,000 laid-off employees, and no attention paid to airport security (House Republican leadership insisted on a continued privatized airport security system, in which checkers and screeners were typically paid no more than seven dollars an hour, with no benefits and little training).

House Republicans also quickly passed a stimulus package that would retroactively eliminate—back to 1986 levels—the minimum tax that America's largest corporations had paid. Under the GOP plan, IBM would get a check from Washington for $1.4 billion, Ford for $1 billion, General Motors for $800 million, Enron for $250 million. More than a dozen other large U.S. companies would receive refunds of at least $100 million for fifteen years of paid corporate taxes. American Airlines and United Airlines, back in the soup line, each expected to receive a check for several hundred million dollars. All in the name of stimulating the economy.

In early October, the administration joined with the U.S. Chamber of Commerce to come to the aid of the nation's largest tobacco companies, which had tried to insert language into antiterrorism legislation to protect them from a spate of pending civil RICO (Racketeer Influenced and Corrupt Organizations Act) lawsuits filed by foreign governments in U.S. courts. They were successful in placing language in the House-passed USA PATRIOT Act that would have taken away foreign governments' ability to bring federal racketeering charges against American tobacco companies that had laundered money in their countries. Despite White House lobbying efforts on behalf of the tobacco companies, Senate Democrats dropped the language.

Then came Fast Track, or, in Bush administration newspeak, Trade Promotion Authority (TPA). Fast track legislation had been so discredited in the eyes of Congress and the public that the Bush administration gave it a new label. This TPA legislation was essentially the same as that implemented back in Nixon's presidency, giving the president the ability to negotiate trade agreements with no labor or environmental safeguards, and with little Congressional input. President Bush planned to use TPA, first and most important, to pass NAFTA-like agreements for all of Latin America. Included in the ambitious agenda were bilateral trade pacts like the Chile Free Trade Agreement, regional agreements like the proposed Central America Free Trade Agreement, and the hemisphere-wide Free Trade Area of the Americas.

United States Trade Representative Robert Zoellick almost immediately linked the president's need for TPA to the fight against terrorism. "America's trade leadership can build a coalition of countries that cherish liberty in all its aspects." In this difficult time, our country needed TPA, he said, "as a cornerstone of international leadership." Calling failure to pass the president's plan in this international time of crisis "a mistake of historical magnitude," Zoellick even compared those who opposed TPA to Gavrilo Princip, the fanatic credited with igniting World War I by assassinating Austrian archduke Franz Ferdinand, implying that Balkan-like "tirades of hate and invective" by TPA opponents could lead to the same kind of "dangerous 'isms'—protectionism, isolationism, authoritarianism" that Princip's murderous act precipitated. Zoellick noted that Princip had been a member of the "shadowy group named the Black Hand," invoking a parallel to the not-so-veiled image of the so-called Black Block anarchists who had roamed the streets of Seattle during the 1999 WTO protests.

Then-Republican majority leader Dick Armey chimed in, echoing Zoellick's words and pointing out "the national security dimension of Fast Track." So did former Mexican president Ernesto Zedillo, a board member of the Cincinnati-based multinational corporation Proctor and Gamble, who proclaimed that environmental, labor, and civic protestors have "an unexpected alliance" with terrorists. David Hartridge, an influential senior official at the WTO Secretariat, openly declared that the September 11 terrorists and activists against corporate-driven globalization shared a propensity for "violent behavior."

Charles Rangel, the senior Democrat on the House Ways and Means Committee and a Korean War combat veteran, angrily responded to Zoellick's efforts to "wrap a trade promotion authority bill in the flag. . . . To appeal to patriotism in an effort to force Congress to move on Fast Track by claiming it is needed to fight terrorism would be laughable if it weren't so serious." Joining Rangel was veteran Ways and Means Democrat Robert Matsui of California, who had voted for every trade agreement since he had arrived in Congress in 1979. Matsui had been rebuffed in trying to work out a more moderate bill with Thomas; Matsui wanted to protect labor and environmental standards and preserve more congressional oversight and input into trade negotiations.

In a November 2001 letter to me and other members of Congress, Leo Gerard, president of the United Steelworkers of America, joined in: "Fast track will not foster national security, nor defend us against other acts of terrorism. Fast track will not find the perpetrators. Fast track will not help those unemployed by the attack or provide an immediate stimulus for the economy."

Fast Track—the 2001 version—was in deep trouble prior to September 11. Despite regular predictions by the White House and Republican congressional leaders that they were going to bring it to a vote in July, then August, then right after Labor Day, it was clear that pro–free trade forces were at least a couple of dozen votes short.

Then came September 11. In the weeks after the attacks, labor and environmental groups—the core of the opposition to Fast Track— were slow to resume their opposition. Most of us thought it unseemly to press our case—with the media, other members of Congress, and the public—in the ensuing weeks after our country's tragedy. But others had a very different view. As the president spoke of national unity and called on Congress to put aside partisan differences, his man on the Ways and Means Committee, Chairman Thomas, led the profiteering by pushing through, with literally no consultation with Democratic leaders on that committee, his TPA bill on a mostly party line vote.

War profiteering was not a new phenomenon in the United States. As a senator, Harry Truman, in disgust, had campaigned against it. Noted financier J.P. Morgan had done it. Howard Zinn, in *A People's History of the United States,* described it this way: "During the Civil War, Morgan bought 5,000 rifles for $3.50 each from an army arsenal, and sold them to a general in the field for $22 each. The rifles were defective and would shoot off the thumbs of the soldiers using them. A congressional committee noted this in the small print of an obscure report, but a federal judge upheld the deal as the fulfillment of a valid legal contract. . . . Morgan had escaped military service in the Civil War by paying $300 to a substitute. So did John D. Rockefeller, Andrew Carnegie, Phillip Armour, Jay Gould, and James Mellon. Mellon's father had written to him that 'a man may be a patriot without risking his own life or sacrificing his health. There are plenty of lives less valuable.' "

While many in the Bush administration and in Congress were

using the events of September 11 to argue for their pre-attack agenda, the government was moving ahead to meet the threats. Lines were longer at the nation's airports, even though fewer people were flying, as the still-private airport security firms asked more questions of passengers and looked more closely at their carry-on luggage. Local governments, with little funding from the federal government, beefed up security at public buildings and municipal water facilities. Municipal electric authorities hired police officers to guard their power plants.

Many of us in Congress who believed our government has starved public health programs in the United States called for a rebuilding of our public health infrastructure. We knew that as a nation we did too little to address foodborne illness, preventive medicine, antibiotic resistance. We wanted more funding for the Centers for Disease Control and Prevention (CDC) and for local and state public health departments—the first line of defense against bioterrorism and against the more common, nagging, persistent public health problems like the flu, low-birth-weight babies, lead poisoning, and the growing disparities in health outcomes based on race and class.

Others who had had little interest in the past in funding the CDC, the nation's (and the world's) preeminent public health organization, discovered the agency had an important role in public health. Unfortunately, their interest in public health seemed to begin—and end—with bioterrorism. They were willing to increase the funding for CDC, and for local and state health departments around the country—at least to respond to anthrax scares. And although the Bush administration had proposed cutting the CDC's budget prior to September 11, it was now willing to spend hundreds of millions of dollars to buy huge quantities of Cipro, an antibiotic used against anthrax, and smallpox vaccines, thus allowing the politically influential prescription drug companies to profiteer a bit.

From the perspective of much of the world, the threat from infectious disease—before and after September 11—looms larger than attacks from terrorists. Some 90,000 children died of malaria in October 2001 as President Bush began to assemble the multinational coalition to fight terrorism. More than 45,000 Africans succumbed to AIDS during the week after September 11, as the United States reeled from the attacks on our country. At least 1,100 people in India died from tuberculosis on the day that anthrax shut down the United States House of Representatives and Speaker Hastert told members of Congress to leave the Capitol.

In early 2003 a new, lethal disease seemed to emerge from nowhere. On February 26 a man was admitted to a hospital in Hanoi with high fever, dry cough, myalgia (muscle soreness), and a mild sore throat. Termed Severe Acute Respiratory Syndrome (SARS) by public health authorities, it spread rapidly through China and around the world; more than 8,000 people were infected worldwide and 774 died. China suffered the most, with 5,327 cases, including 349 deaths. Canada, hardest hit among the rich countries, reported a total of 251 cases, including 43 deaths. The world's underfunded and understaffed public health community fought back valiantly and effectively, but was generally unprepared to deal with the SARS virus—a lesson for the American public that was all too familiar to these experts.

Trade policy figures prominently in the spread of infectious disease. As Nicaraguans lose their farms because of World Bank–induced plummeting coffee prices, they flock to refugee camps and urban areas, dramatically increasing their chances of contracting tuberculosis, HIV, or hepatitis. As the World Bank forces structural adjustment on some of the globe's poorest nations in order to increase exports, cuts in public health spending devastate an already exceedingly inadequate and fragile health-care infrastructure.

As administration lobbyists were unsuccessful in their efforts to link expanded trade and terrorism, Trade Representative Zoellick told Congress that the United States would be embarrassed if the new round of trade talks, the WTO ministerial in Qatar, found the U.S. government unable to empower their trade negotiators with the fast-track TPA. But Zoellick's and Thomas's pleas—whether in the name of antiterrorism, or to protect the position of the United States as the world's leading trading nation—fell on deaf congressional ears; the administration simply could not round up the votes before the WTO's November 2001 meeting in Qatar.

Qatar was a story in itself. Proponents of globalization were delighted with the choice of the city of Doha for the ministerial because its location and its government guaranteed a safer, more peaceful, and quieter environment for the hundreds of finance ministers and heads of state who were attending. Qatar was the exact opposite of open, accessible Seattle. Visas were hard to come by. Police protection was virtually airtight. The Qatar government was, to put it mildly, intolerant of dissent.

Those were the same reasons that antiglobalization activists were unhappy with the location. Qatar—to those of us who oppose unregulated global commerce—sent all the wrong messages to people around the world. According to the *CIA Factbook*, the government has granted suffrage only in municipal elections. The organization Human Rights Watch was critical of the selection of Qatar because its government does not recognize the right of freedom to assembly. Although Al Jazeera, the Middle-Eastern broadcasting network, is located in Qatar, freedom of speech is severely limited, according to the United States Department of State. The country's government bans political demonstrations, and it officially prohibits public worship by non-Muslims. According to the United States State Department's *Country Reports*, women occupy a strictly subservient legal and social role in Qatar society, not much different from their condition under the Taliban in Afghanistan.

To the trade ministers, Qatar made much more sense than Seattle in 1999 or another accessible Western location. For example, the G8 summit in Geneva, Switzerland, attracted more than 200,000 overwhelmingly peaceful protestors who figuratively forced the meeting doors open, looking for a seat at the table. Protestors around the globe—more than a million of them in more than fifty demonstrations in a dozen countries in the previous eighteen months—demanded something different from these nations, and succeeded in pushing the G8 leaders to place African poverty at the top of the agenda, an agenda that historically ignored the needs of the poorest people in the most impoverished nations.

In many ways, though, Qatar *was* the perfect place for a meeting of the World Trade Organization. U.S. corporations have shown their interest in investing increasingly more in developing authoritarian countries rather than in developing democracies. Western investors and large multinational corporations have demonstrated a clear preference for nations such as China over democratic societies like India, and for dictatorships like Qatar over democracies like Taiwan. After all, workers in China and Qatar do not organize labor unions, do not demand higher wages and better worker conditions, and do not enjoy freedom of religion, freedom of speech, and freedom of association, all of which can get in the way of profits.

One very good thing came out of Qatar, however. Zoellick agreed to provisions that allowed poor nations greater access to cheap generic drugs manufactured in developing countries to respond to public health emergencies and more everyday public health needs. This was a significant move, since for years the United States trade representative had threatened economic retribution against nations such as India, which houses huge generic drug manufacturers, and against countries such as Thailand and South Africa, which want to purchase more inexpensive generic drugs made in the developing world. James Love, who directs the Consumer Project on Technology, exalted, "For once, the poor beat the rich."

But what one hand gives, the other tries to take away. The Thomas trade bill, in granting trade promotion authority to the president, also contained a provision strengthening the monopoly powers of the American pharmaceutical industry and giving their patents greater authority in international sales and promotions. The Thomas TPA provision "to achieve the elimination of government measures such as price controls and reference pricing" could override the overwhelming votes in the House in the summer of 2001 and again in 2003 for bills allowing Americans to re-import prescription drugs and save substantial amounts of money. TPA denies nations like Mexico and Canada the ability to negotiate less expensive drug prices. Many Americans actually go to Canada and Mexico to buy the same drugs they get at their corner drugstore at one-third or one-fourth, or even one-fifth, the price. Rather than allowing U.S. retailers to purchase drugs from Canadian or Mexican wholesalers and pass the huge savings on to American consumers, or allowing the U.S. government to purchase prescription drugs in large quantities to sell at cost to America's elderly, President Bush asked Congress—using the vehicle of Trade Promotion Authority—to force our trading partners to raise prices on prescription drugs.* Never passing up a chance to assist the nation's drug companies, the Bush administration used the 2003 Medicare legislation to discourage less expensive mail order drugs

---

* This was not the first time that a President Bush had gone to bat for the big drug companies. A decade earlier, the first President Bush had done the same, in the context of an international trade agreement, for the United States pharmaceutical industry. When he was negotiating the North American Free Trade Agreement with the Canadians, he demanded that our neighbor to the north eliminate its compulsory licensing practices in determining drug prices. Although Ottawa capitulated to Bush, the Canadians, to their credit, found other ways to keep drug prices down for their citizens.

and senior citizen bus trips to Canada (which I arranged in my district) to buy prescription drugs.

Zoellick's and the U.S. trade delegation's first act in Doha was to put our antidumping laws on the negotiating table, in effect scuttling one of the few tools that U.S. workers have to level the playing field in trade law. A week earlier, the House had passed—with strong support from both political parties—a resolution urging President Bush and his trade negotiators to keep U.S. antidumping laws, import surge protection laws, and countervailing duty laws off the negotiating table. These laws imposed protective tariffs on commodities such as steel to safeguard against surging imports on U.S. markets—goods exported to the United States at below their domestic market cost, and goods supported by government subsidies or programs which unfairly benefited overseas producers. Even Congressman Matsui, a Democrat with a free-trade résumé, said that Zoellick's action "undermined the whole premise of our participation" in the WTO.

Others also felt betrayed. Then-House minority leader Richard Gephardt (D-Missouri) said, "We are in the middle of a steel crisis in this country, and our own government has hurt our efforts to fight back." And as LTV announced closure of its mills in Cleveland and other cities across the nation, steelworkers meeting in Cleveland questioned our trade policy, and argued for protecting a vibrant steel industry for national security purposes.

Zoellick also made it clear, from his first day in Qatar, that this was no Clinton delegation. Although the United States, during the last days of the Clinton administration, had positioned itself in Seattle in support of labor rights, Zoellick said no to trade and labor rights linkage and opposed even the toothless declaration on labor rights agreed to in Singapore in 1996. The five conditions of the International Labor Organization—the right to associate, the right to organize and bargain collectively, the prohibition of forced labor, a ban on child labor, and the outlawing of discrimination—would not be on the American agenda. The Qatar ministerial came and went with minimal press coverage, just as the trade ministers had planned. But free trade remained at the top of President Bush's agenda.

Before Thanksgiving 2001, then-Republican majority leader Dick Armey announced that the vote on Trade Promotion Authority/Fast Track would take place on December 6. As usual, you didn't need a scorecard to identify the players on each side. In support of Trade Promotion Authority/Fast Track were the president, the Republican leadership, the CEOs of America's most powerful and wealthiest corporations, and almost every major newspaper publisher and editor in the country. In opposition were House Democratic leaders, labor unions, environmental organizations, human rights groups, and—according to every major published poll—a strong majority of the public. With the power and influence arrayed against us, as on every trade bill, those of us in opposition knew that we had our work cut out for us.

We used the familiar arguments with other members, at news conferences, on talk shows, and in speeches at home: the trade deficit had swelled from $38 billion the year that NAFTA negotiations had been completed to $482 billion in 2002; the U.S. economy was experiencing the longest decline in industrial-output activity since the Great Depression levels of 1932; we had lost more than 2.5 million manufacturing jobs in the first thirty months of the George W. Bush administration, one out of six manufacturing jobs in my home state of Ohio.

In the developing world, things were much worse. The income gap between the fifth of the world's people living in the richest countries and the fifth living in the poorest doubled between 1960 and 1990—from a 30-1 ratio to 60-1. By 1998, it had ballooned to 78-1, the United Nations' *Human Development Report* announced, with

100 million more poor people in the developing world today than ten years earlier. The number of people living on less than $2 a day outside of China rose from 1.9 billion in 1990 to about 2.3 billion today.

As the vote drew nearer, the appeals to patriotism and to "do this for the president" became more frequent. President Bush himself called or personally met with more than three dozen representatives, asserting that he needed members of Congress—especially Republicans—to support TPA to fight this war on terrorism. Two Florida Republicans were invited on Air Force One so the president would have an opportunity to lobby them, meet their objections, and cut a (likely protectionist) deal. Secretary of Commerce Don Evans said that he met with more than one hundred members to try to convince them to support TPA. In a series of meetings at the White House, the president promised House Republicans protection—via the free-trade bill—for textiles, citrus, apparel, and specialty crops, but mostly, the president's pitch was patriotism. Ultraconservative Bob Barr, a Georgia Republican, said that Bush told him, " 'As president, I need your vote for our nation's security.' " Barr, who had never been a free trader, obliged.

Matsui, Rangel, and Michigan's Sandy Levin, the senior Democrat on the House Ways and Means subcommittee on trade, suggested language that would have provided substantive labor and environmental standards—not as mere window dressing, but as real protections in the core agreement. "It's no longer whether you are for or against trade," Matsui said, "it's how you manage trade."

Across the country, grassroots opponents of free trade had worked ceaselessly for a year to try to derail Trade Promotion Authority. In Ohio, for example, John Ryan, Barbara Janis, Linda Romanik, and David Prentice knew what they had to do. The four northeast Ohio labor activists saw Trade Promotion Authority as another threat to the social and economic well-being of union members. They me-

thodically directed calls, letters, e-mail, and faxes from their union
members to the three undecided congressmen in northeast Ohio.
They organized meetings and rallies and demonstrations. They wrote
articles in union publications and held news conferences to attract
coverage in mainstream, corporate-owned media like the *Plain
Dealer* in Cleveland and the *Akron Beacon-Journal*.

They also knew that the industrial base in their part of Ohio was in
jeopardy, and that Congress was about to make things worse. The events
of September 11 accelerated the downturn, but the signs were evident
months before: Auto companies threatened major layoffs. Smaller
manufacturers in Elyria and Akron and Cleveland were laying off
twelve people, twenty people, thirty-two people. The steel mill in Lorain, once a company with 12,000 jobs, was in trouble. LTV, the third-
largest integrated steelmaker in the United States, filed for bankruptcy
in December 2000 and announced in November 2001 that it was going
to close the mill (soon after the top two executives took in excess of $1
million bonuses for themselves). There was a lot riding on this vote.
Groups like the Northeast Ohio Coalition for American Manufacturing were meeting with their members of Congress, demanding that
Congress enact a manufacturing policy, asking for better trade deals
and a tax policy that targeted small, domestic manufacturing.

I organized a November 2001 meeting between major environmental groups and leading environmental members of Congress in
Democratic whip David Bonior's office; the group included George
Miller, Peter DeFazio, Mike Capuano, Jan Schakowsky, Lynn Woolsey,
and Lloyd Doggett. Prior to the vote on Trade Promotion Authority,
the environmental movement as a whole had never fought against a
trade bill. After our meeting, in a letter to House members, the League
of Conservation Voters announced that it would likely include members' votes on this issue on its environmental scorecard, an important

consideration for many—especially Democrats and northeastern Republicans—who proudly point to their pro-environment voting records at election time.

The weekly trade whip meetings to count votes and organize our forces began in mid-October 2001. We knew, almost from the start, that we had at least 160 Democratic votes in opposition to Trade Promotion Authority. Only seven Democrats—Carson from Oklahoma, Dicks from Washington, Dooley from California, Tanner from Tennessee, Moran from Virginia, Hall from Texas, and Jefferson from Louisiana—were publicly committed to vote for the bill. We also knew that another ten would be exceedingly difficult to hold. Bonior, Matsui, and I led the whip effort and we knew that we had to keep the Democratic numbers below about twenty-five. Too many Republicans would wilt under pressure from the president.

Amazingly, we could find no Republican—even though fifty-eight Republican members who were still in Congress had voted against granting fast-track authority to President Clinton—to organize a whip effort in opposition to the Trade Promotion Authority legislation. It was clear that at least half of those Republicans who had established themselves as opponents of free trade would drop their opposition when the appeal came from a Republican president. A call from President Bush, especially with an appeal to patriotism, would cause lots of Republicans to change their vote and support TPA.

Thousands of calls, perhaps tens of thousands of calls, came into the offices of the thirty to forty undecided Republican and Democratic members. They came from business lobbyists, their corporate clients, and their executives; on the other side came significantly more calls from labor union members, environmental activists, and human rights advocates.

Other efforts continued around the country. Both sides ran radio and television ads in the districts of undecided members. Democratic

Majority Leader Gephardt met with small groups of undecided members to try to persuade them to oppose TPA. Ohio Democrat Marcy Kaptur and other agriculture experts and farm-state opponents to TPA buttonholed their colleagues on the deleterious effects of trade agreements on agriculture. Freshmen Hilda Solis (D-California) and Stephen Lynch (D-Massachusetts) were earning their spurs on this vote, as they dutifully took names at whip meetings and talked with members whom they were getting to know. Lloyd Doggett, Tom Allen, and I spoke with a couple dozen Republicans about a provision inserted into TPA by America's drug companies that would have given them a greater ability to negotiate even higher prescription drug prices.

On the day of the vote, we knew that the Republicans were a few votes short. We were going to lose as many as twenty-five Democrats (we hoped to keep it under that number), but we thought we had a chance to get as many as twenty-seven or twenty-eight Republicans. There was some speculation that Republican leaders—strong TPA advocates to the person—might pull the bill off the floor because they were not sure that they were going to win. But they decided to roll the dice.

After the debate, the roll call began. Usually lasting the fifteen minutes on the scoreboard clock, plus another couple of minutes to make sure that everyone has had a chance to vote, the roll call this time was surely going to last a lot longer. It was clear that the Republican leadership was still a handful of votes short, perhaps as many as five. Seventeen minutes turned into twenty, then twenty-five; congresswoman Kaptur, who always has a sense of fair play, demanded that the roll call be concluded and the votes stand. "Regular order! Regular order!" she shouted. All, of course, to no avail. Then thirty minutes, then thirty-five, forty, and we were still ahead (by a vote of 210–214). It was now past three in the morning and most of the nation was asleep. Political cynicism kicked in.

South Carolina Republican Jim DeMint—representing a textile area and publicly opposing Fast Track, and who had actually already cast a no vote—yielded to the pressure tactics of Republican leadership. He secured a letter from House Republican leaders promising assistance in protecting, in a *free-trade* agreement, textile companies in South Carolina. DeMint went down to the well of the House chamber—in view of everyone—and switched his vote, to the cheers of rank-and-file Republicans and the jeers of many Democrats. (Most members of the House have seen letters like that, with promises from presidents to address specific, parochial concerns. We have also seen the promises inevitably evaporate after the vote is cast; within days of DeMint's switch, the evaporation process had already begun. Thomas, the Republican Ways and Means chairman from California, told people privately the next day that he was determined to break the promise that Speaker Hastert and Whip DeLay had made to DeMint.)

After DeMint brandished his letter (the roll call by then had been held open for twenty extra minutes), four other Republicans came down to the well to cast their votes in support. One of them, Representative Robin Hayes, who was actually whipping against Fast Track during the first minutes of the roll call vote, had tears in his eyes as he succumbed to the pressure of Majority Whip Tom DeLay and GOP leadership. The *Wall Street Journal,* an enforcer of Republican Party discipline and free-trade cheerleader, said that Hayes was "visibly shaken" by his vote switch. The vote was finally decided, in the words of former Reagan trade official Robert E. Lighthizer, "after old-fashioned arm-twisting . . . and a strike of the gavel before opponents had time to act." Lindsay Graham, a gutsy South Carolina Republican, opposed granting Fast Track to Clinton and again opposed giving it to Bush. The morning after the vote, he ruefully told me, "Several Republicans lost their jobs last night."

Fully 90 percent of the Democrats opposed TPA, a testament to the work of an energized labor and environmental movement, the Democratic whip operation, and the work of Bob Matsui. All six members from northeast Ohio voted no—Tubbs Jones, Kucinich, Regula, Sawyer, LaTourette, and I—clearly a victory for the organizational efforts of Barbara Janis, John Ryan, Linda Romanik, Dave Prentice, and others in Cleveland, Akron, and Lorain.

The passage of TPA was assured, however, because of the huge number of House Republicans supporting the bill. No fewer than 194 Republicans voted for the bill; only 23 opposed it. Two-thirds of the fifty-eight Republicans who voted against Fast Track for President Clinton turned around and supported granting that same authority to President Bush. Several Republican members—Hart, Platts, and English from Pennsylvania; Everett and Riley from Alabama; Shimkus of Illinois; Ney of Ohio—were a disappointment, mostly because of the economic devastation in the steel industry brought on by foreign imports. Others from textile areas, which have experienced maybe even more disastrous economic woes than steel—Ballenger, Hayes, Burr, and Myrick from North Carolina; Henry Brown and DeMint from South Carolina; Barr and Deal from Georgia—were equally disappointing. But the biggest disappointments of all were those members who dutifully trooped to the House floor night after night in 1993 during the NAFTA debate and in 1997 and 1998 when Congress considered granting fast-track authority to President Clinton. They seemed to put party above their fair-trade principles, responding instead to President Bush's call to so-called patriotism. They included Duncan Hunter of California; Lincoln Diaz-Balart, Cliff Stearns, and Ileana Ros-Lehtinen of Florida; Terry Everett of Alabama; and Mark Souder of Indiana (who was not in Congress during NAFTA but was rightly critical of Clinton on that issue and on Fast Track).

Respected, longtime *Washington Post* columnist David Broder called the 215–214 passage of Trade Promotion Authority "a nakedly

partisan vote." It broke, he said, the bipartisanship which had generally characterized trade debates and trade policy in the past. Few
issues—with about 90 percent of each party going their party's way—
were this partisan in Congress, and trade had never been. Broder
blamed Republican leadership, fingering Republican Whip Tom
DeLay as the main culprit. Martin Tolchin, publisher of the Capitol
Hill newspaper *The Hill,* attacked the unprecedented twenty-three-
minute delay that kept the vote open and the "frantic last-minute
arm-twisting, horse trading and blatant political bribery" by Republican leaders on the House floor.

Little did we know the precedent that was set that night. The following year, contentious, middle-of-the-night votes became com-
monplace. Never before has the House of Representatives operated in
such secrecy: In 2003, under the cover of darkness, it happened almost every month. At 2:54 A.M. on a Friday in March, the House cut
veterans' benefits by three votes. At 2:39 A.M. on a Friday in April, the
House slashed education and health care by five votes. At 1:56 A.M. on
a Friday in May, the House passed the "Leave No Millionaire Behind"
tax-cut bill by a handful of votes. At 2:33 A.M. on a Friday in June, the
House passed the Medicare privatization and prescription drug bill
by one vote. At 12:57 A.M. on a Friday in July, the House eviscerated
Head Start by one vote. Then, after returning from summer recess,
the House voted $87 billion for Iraq at 12:12 A.M. on a Friday in Octo-
ber. Finally, closing out the year, the House passed the final Medicare
bill—after a *three-hour* roll call—at 5:55 on a Saturday morning. Always in the middle of the night. Always after the press had passed
their deadlines. Always after the American people had turned off the
news and gone to bed.

Quite a precedent TPA had set. Columnist Broder said that there
were more lobbyists lined up outside the House chamber and on the
sidewalk to the Capitol than he had ever seen in his several decades

covering Congress. Republicans—almost 90 percent of them—rallied around the Republican president and came to the aid of their corporate allies, many of whom contributed large sums of money to the National Republican Congressional Committee and to individual members. When asked about the near-loss a few days later at one of Washington's most expensive restaurants, United States Chamber of Commerce president and Bush ally Thomas Donohue quipped, "A one-vote margin is all that we could afford."

Democrats—in even higher percentages—supported their traditional labor, environment, and human rights allies. Most Democrats, in the end, just did not trust a president who had, in less than a year in office, attempted to weaken environmental and labor standards in the United States domestic economy. Why would we expect him to enforce or strengthen those standards in a global economy?

3

Myth 3: Free Trade Is an Extension of American Values Abroad

It's not whether we add more to the abundance of those who have
much; it is whether we provide enough for those who have too little.
—*Franklin Delano Roosevelt*

The engine of U.S. economic growth has produced great wealth in our country and for many people around the world. Yet our own history tells us that it should come as no surprise that American business has shown little interest in exporting our democratic ideals.

For one hundred years it has been a struggle—in the United States and in every successful industrial democracy in the world—to make capitalism work for all of society. Coal miners took canaries into the mines to alert them to dangerous fumes that might kill them because government was not there to help. Upton Sinclair's *The Jungle,* published in 1906, chronicled worker exploitation, company antiunion efforts, and threats to public health. That time, when a shocked President Theodore Roosevelt invited the author to the White House, government *was* there to help. Sinclair's book, and the efforts of social workers, union organizers, and other activists, convinced President Roosevelt and Congress to enact food safety measures and eventually more protections for workers and consumers.

But none of these advances in the public interest ever happened without a battle; they always took place in the face of intractable business opposition. Even something as ostensibly simple as labeling the contents of many food items was—finally, after many years—enacted in 1991 over the objections of the food manufacturers and processors.

"With all the fervor of an Ezekiel," the *New York Times Book Review* wrote in 1962, Rachel Carson, in *Silent Spring,* did for the environment what *The Jungle* did for food safety. *Silent Spring* served as a catalyst for a nascent environmental movement by alerting the American public to the indiscriminate use of pesticides that constituted a hazard to human beings, animals, and the ecosystem. The *New York Times Book Review* opined that *Silent Spring* was "a cry to the reading public to help curb private and public programs which by use of poisons will end up destroying life on earth." Others were not so kind to the fifty-five-year-old former U.S. Fish and Wildlife Service publications editor. The chemical industry, especially Monsanto, savaged her. *Time* magazine belittled her "oversimplifications and downright errors. . . . Many of her scary generalizations—and there are lots of them—are patently unsound." Before her death from cancer two years later, however, almost all scientists but those on the payrolls of agribusiness and the chemical industry lauded her work and her contribution to public health. The book became a best-seller, and the American environmental movement took off.

Today in the United States there is undoubtedly a broad consensus that we need rules governing our free enterprise system: strong environmental standards, enforceable worker safety and minimum wage laws, and solid food safety and consumer protection regulations. Americans intuitively understand that our enhanced quality of life and ever-increasing life expectancy—from forty-five in 1900 to almost eighty today—are in large part due to public health laws, food and workplace safety rules, and environmental regulations.

In fact, according to Dr. Jeffrey P. Koplan, director of the Centers for Disease Control and Prevention in Atlanta in the late 1990s, "We have gained 35 years of life" this century. He went on to say that only about "five of these 'extra' years can be attributed to advances in clinical medicine. . . . Public health can take the credit for the other 30 years, thanks to improvements in sanitation, health education, the development of effective vaccines, and other hallmarks of our field." These advances were not the result of corporate generosity or philanthropy. Most have come from federal, state, and local government initiatives—from capital expenditures on infrastructure, to direct services from local public health authorities, to regulatory rules on food safety, clean air, and safe drinking water.

But it has never been easy. Conservative legislatures and Congresses have always—from the early years of our country—worked to enhance corporate power at the behest of the most privileged in society, usually at the expense of democratic, elected governments and always to the detriment of workers, consumers, and the environment. In the fall of 1994, conservatives in the United States Congress presented to the American people the "Contract with America," a blueprint to deregulate much of the United States' economy. It proposed rolling back environmental laws, weakening worker safety standards, depressing wages, and eviscerating food and consumer safety protections.

After the 1994 elections, in which Republicans won the majority in the House of Representatives, several Republicans backed efforts to privatize the national park system by selling parks to corporations,* charge admission prices to government buildings such as the Capitol,† privatize Medicare by creating Medical Savings Accounts and encouraging insurance company HMOs to take over the system, and privatize Social Security by allowing Wall Street access to investment dollars.

The Republican strategy was threefold: first, weaken environmental, food safety, and worker protection laws; second, cut the funding for enforcement of the laws that were still in place; and third, take away the victims' right to sue the manufacturers of dangerous products. At the same time, Speaker Gingrich and House Republicans argued that more and more federal authority should be turned over to the states, and that the one-size-fits-all model was too inflexible and heavy-handed. They chose to ignore the historical evidence, however, that the federal government has served as a counterweight to corporate power. Only the federal government has the wherewithal to face down corporate polluters, antiworker manufacturers, and wealthy interest groups.

Since the eighteenth century, after the Articles of Confederation were replaced and the loose organization of states was turned into a more centralized constitutional system, the American people have known that a strong federal government would do a better job— through national roads and canals, the Northwest Ordinance, land grant colleges, Social Security, the school lunch program, Medicare, the Environmental Protection Agency—of addressing national concerns like fighting poverty, increasing opportunity, providing health

---

* Perhaps we could have the Philip Morris Smoky Mountains and the Liberty Taco Bell.

† "Think of the wear on the marble steps when you count the number of feet that have walked on it, and the brushing up against the walls," one Republican aide who supported charging admission chortled.

care for the elderly, enforcing civil rights laws, cleaning up the Great Lakes, and building an interstate highway system. That is why a more moderate Senate rejected most of these proposals from the Gingrich House. People were generally satisfied with a system that generates wealth, as America's free enterprise system does, yet checks the excesses of capitalism such as environmental degradation and worker exploitation. In *The Affluent Society*, John Kenneth Galbraith wrote:

> Capitalism, left to its own devices, doesn't work properly; it excludes the poor, ruins the environment, and fails to deliver enough collectively produced goods, such as roads, reservoirs, schools, and hospitals.

To be sure, the market does many things very well; it generates wealth and raises our standard of living. Private industry is the dynamic engine of job growth in our society. But equally surely, the free market does not protect the environment or provide health care to the uninsured. A market economy with no public safeguards will create a vast gulf between those who reap the rewards and those who are left with none.

Robert Kuttner, in his seminal 1997 book on the perils of privatization, *Everything for Sale*, pointed out that there are many social and economic goods that the free market simply does not produce. Free markets, he explained, do not invest adequately in research, so government must step in—either to directly fund research or provide incentives to the private sector to undertake that responsibility. Government has made our society wealthier, by investing in airports and railroads, canals and highways, soil conservation and lake preservation, scientific research and the Internet, Head Start and higher education. Almost no one in or out of Washington disagrees with the public benefits brought to the American people by the National Institutes of Health and the Centers for Disease Control and Prevention, two federal agencies that have provided billions of scientific research dollars that have led to major breakthroughs in medical care and public health. Much of the research carried out by these and other federal agencies has led to huge advances—and profits—in the private sector, especially in the biotechnology and pharmaceutical industries.

Similarly, health and safety regulation—to assure clean air and safe food, to ensure worker safety and airline safety—has meant decades of prosperity. For example, the United States Environmental Protection Agency estimated in 1996 that Clean Air Act compliance cost $436 billion over twenty years. The benefits—in improved health, reductions in lost workdays, agricultural productivity, and reduced clean-up benefits—were at least $2.3 trillion and perhaps as much as $14 trillion. "The zenith," Kuttner wrote, "of the era of regulation—the postwar boom—was the most successful era of American capitalism."

Even the more conservative Bush II White House, which has shown little regard for environmental regulation, acknowledged that the benefits to society of strong environmental rules outweigh the costs. The White House's Office of Management and Budget (OMB) released a report in September 2003 that looked specifically at Clean Air Act programs from 1992 through 2002. The OMB found that industry, states, and municipalities spent about $25 billion to comply with clean air regulations during that decade, but the analysis estimated that the benefits from cleaner air—such as reductions in hospitalization and emergency room visits, premature deaths, and lost workdays—exceeded $190 billion.

Under the guise of free trade, however, the largest corporations in the world are expanding their power, undermining freely elected governments and co-opting authoritative regimes on every continent. As multinationals expand their control over the international economy, governments' ability to clean their air, ensure the safety of their workers, provide for a pure food supply, and sustain a decent standard of living atrophies. "Megacompanies," wrote former undersecretary of Commerce and now Yale School of Management dean Jeffrey Garten, "exercise huge power over politicians when it comes to such issues as environmental standards . . . and tax policy."

For decades, every session of Congress has featured environmentalists and public health advocates in a battle with industry. Occasionally the environment wins. Sometimes public health wins. Usually industry—better funded with far greater access to corporate-controlled media—wins. But as a result of a series of often small and occasionally large victories for public health, life expectancy in the United States has increased more than thirty years in the last century. In the global economy, however, the polluters almost never lose. Decades of efforts in nation after nation by citizen activists and progressive elected officials to protect air and water quality, to force employers to pay livable wages, to ensure safe working conditions, and to raise standards of living are undermined by corporate greed.

Yet some argue that those rules that govern our domestic economy are unnecessary in the new global economic order. What makes sense for the United States at home is not important in the global economy, globalization enthusiasts assure us. Somehow, safety, wage, and environmental standards will evolve in country after country around the world, they assert, without any legal checks on the free market.

In 1997 President Clinton and Speaker Gingrich submitted to Congress legislation giving the president fast-track authority to negotiate additional trade agreements. H.R. 2621, introduced by then–House Ways and Means chairman Bill Archer, did not look much different from the deregulation provisions of the Contract with

America: it made no allowance for the environment, for worker rights, and for food safety.* It was global economics with no rules. This unregulated global economy, unacceptable to people like President Clinton in our domestic economy, is for some reason acceptable in the international economy. "We're not for trickle-down domestically," Massachusetts Democrat Barney Frank countered, "why should we be for trickle-down internationally?"

The Clinton/Gingrich/Archer bill, introduced in Congress on October 7, 1997, was similar to legislation introduced in January 1997 by ultraconservative Texas Republican senator Phil Gramm. The Gramm bill prohibited the inclusion of any environmental or labor standards in any trade agreement legislation that was negotiated under fast-track procedures. In other words, labor rights, environmental protections, and food safety standards could not be included in any agreements that the United States negotiated under fast-track negotiating authority with any Latin American country.

In contrast, a decade earlier, a Democratic Congress had passed stronger, more accountable fast-track legislation. In granting fast-track negotiating authority to President Reagan in 1988, the House and Senate set core labor standards as a condition of market access (the only way to really accomplish any of these standards) as a congressionally mandated negotiating objective. United States Trade Representative Carla Hills and the Bush-appointed U.S. trade negotiators, however, simply ignored their congressional directives in the NAFTA negotiations and in the General Agreement on Tariffs and Trade negotiations. Then Congress ultimately acquiesced in an up-or-down vote on the North American Free Trade Agreement.

The Uruguay round of the General Agreement on Tariffs and

---

* Bill Archer, a very conservative Republican from Texas, was elected in 1970 to fill the House seat vacated by George H. W. Bush.

Trade at first drew little attention in Congress, among the media, and from the general public. Then, in September 1994, during congressional deliberations on GATT (which would become the WTO), fifty-one leaders of news organizations sent a letter to President Clinton denouncing the secrecy and inaccessibility of the trade organization's deliberations as "an affront to the democratic traditions of this nation." Earlier that summer more than thirty state attorneys general and other state officials protested to the president that the organization's secret tribunals would infringe upon state sovereignty. The opposition to GATT—from prominent historians like James Mac-Gregor Bums to social activists like Gloria Steinem and Phyllis Schlafly, from native American tribes to labor, environmental, and consumer groups—went mostly unreported by the media and unnoticed by the public. The opponents of GATT were dismissed as protectionists, Luddites, members of the Flat Earth Society. Most of the criticisms of GATT simply fell on deaf ears; in fact, a *New York Times* reporter wrote shortly after the 1994 vote, "Over the past year the administration tried desperately to keep anyone from noticing GATT." And the media seemed to comply.

The fears that WTO would also operate in secret with little public accountability were quickly realized. By its very nature, the World Trade Organization is an undemocratic organization that is staffed exclusively by unelected bureaucrats. Its dispute resolution panels, a sort of Supreme Court of trade disputes, typically consist of trade lawyers and economists not accountable to the public. These panels rule on issues of public health and safety, environmental laws, and other trade disputes. The panel's exclusionary administrative practices and resistance to amicus briefs contribute to its secrecy.

The panel's decisions, with no public input allowed from health or environmental organizations, are announced to the public, but the panels do not reveal the process surrounding the outcome. Most governments have been unwilling to release publicly their submissions to the dispute panels, and the WTO itself refuses to make public any records of dispute proceedings, so it is nearly impossible for affected groups—the media, environmental organizations, human rights groups, trade unions, individual citizens—to understand the logic behind the dispute panel's decision. The findings can be overturned only by a unanimous vote of all WTO members, which will likely never happen, because the country that won the decision would obviously not appeal. Any appeal by those contesting WTO decisions is also secretive, being decided by a different three-judge panel. The process is exceedingly slow and laborious and can take years to resolve.

Dr. Jeff Sachs, a Harvard economist, said, "International institutions like IMF and WTO have a deep democratic deficit." The intent was never anything else. As Susan Aaronson of the National Policy Association pointed out, "The WTO is an organization of governments; there is no place there for civil society." To join the WTO, countries must, as economist Pat Choate wrote, "agree to alter their domestic laws, regulations, and administrative practices to conform to WTO agreements and dispute rulings. The only recourse to noncompliance is for the offending government to pay compensation to afflicted parties." Author William Greider called the WTO "a private club for deal-making among the most powerful interests, portrayed as a public institution searching for international 'consensus.' The WTO aspires, in effect, to create a bill of rights for capital, crafted one case at a time by the corporate lawyers filing their confidential pleadings in Geneva. It is not hyperbole when critics say the system defends property rights but dismisses human rights and common social concerns as irrelevant to trade."

The public began to notice that global trade rules were being written by faceless foreign finance ministers, unknown trade officials from the United States, and nameless corporate leaders of the world's largest companies. The more the public learned about U.S. trade policy, the less they liked it. They were finding out that our clean air laws were weakened when the WTO sided with the state-run Venezuelan oil company's contention that U.S. regulations against gasoline contaminants were too stringent. They were learning that our endangered species and animal protection laws were compromised when foreign tuna and shrimp interests brought actions against the United States in the World Trade Organization. They were hearing that our Great Lakes water may one day be treated as any other commodity and become available for bulk sales by the tankerful to any country wanting water. And they suspected that our laws, which keep subsidized goods, artificially cheap imports, and unfair import surges from flooding U.S. markets, could be legally challenged in the WTO. In short, the American public and the United States Congress were finding out that the promises made to us about trade were broken.

And the world watched the demonstrations against the World Trade Organization in Seattle and Geneva and Cancún, and learned as well. Some of the European Union's most important food safety laws were challenged by the U.S. government on behalf of our domestic beef industry and overturned by the WTO. Other laws, passed by the elected legislatures of sovereign nations to protect the public, were struck down.

In fact, as the leaders of the eight nations gathered in Geneva, the WTO—celebrating its eighth year—still had an almost perfect record; every democratically attained environmental and public health rule or law challenged in the WTO had been overturned except one.* Under the rules and guidelines of the World Trade Organization, these laws—public health laws enacted by democratically

---

* The WTO used convoluted and technical arguments to uphold France's ban on asbestos, thus avoiding a politically deadly decision if it had struck down this worker safety law.

elected governments to protect the well-being of their citizens—were all considered nontariff barriers to trade: illegal trade barriers that must be eliminated or changed under WTO rules.

The WTO's three-judge dispute resolution panels—the ones that in almost every instance have classified environmental and health standards as illegal barriers to trade—typically consist of economists and trade lawyers, not scientists, not physicians, not public health advocates, not elected officials who are accountable to the public. The public became increasingly aware, thanks in large part to the "Battle in Seattle," that our clean air and water regulations and our food safety laws are increasingly subject to the whims of the unelected and unaccountable trade lawyers at the WTO.

Conversely, in the United States, agencies to which Congress delegates quasi-legislative authority must, under the Administrative Procedures Act, give reasons for their actions and decisions. Hearings are accessible to the public, comment periods are available, and sunshine laws apply. The World Trade Organization has no such obligations.

The marchers in Seattle and the protestors in Geneva believed that if trade laws protect intellectual property rights, they should also protect the environment. They believed that if our trade laws protect patents, they should protect our food safety. And they believed that if our trade laws protect Hollywood movies, they should protect worker rights. The delegates inside and the public outside the meetings—and I was part of both in Seattle—heard the depth of passion and the breadth of support for enforceable standards to help workers and to protect the environment, and for a trade policy as interested in American values of fairness as in corporate profits.

A University of Maryland poll, taken after the Seattle meetings in early December 1999, found that 78 percent of Americans believed that the WTO should consider labor standards and the environment in trade decisions. An emphatic 93 percent said that "countries that are part of international trade agreements should be required to maintain minimum standards for working conditions." And 74 percent agreed that "if people in other countries are making products that we use, this creates a moral obligation for us to make efforts to ensure that they do not have to work in harsh or unsafe conditions." Only 23 percent agreed that "it is not for us to judge what the working conditions should be in another country."

In another survey, the Zogby Poll, which was released two weeks after the Seattle talks, an overwhelming 83 percent said that, when entering trade agreements, the United States should "insist the other country meet environmental, job security and labor condition standards." And 66 percent believed that the United States should insist on better human rights and religious freedom from China before admitting it to the WTO.

More recently, as the presidential race began to heat up and Democratic candidates were focusing on President Bush's economic performance, support for free trade fell even further. In a University of Maryland poll in January 2004, respondents were given three options; only 20 percent said, "I support the growth of international trade in principle and I approve of the way the U.S. is going about expanding international trade," while 53 percent said, "I support the growth of international trade in principle, but I am not satisfied with the way the U.S. government is dealing with the effects of trade on American jobs, the poor in other countries, and the environment," and 18 percent opposed the growth of trade.

The Seattle meeting instilled in many Americans an intuitive understanding that we had been here before, that the WTO represents another chapter in the essential American struggle—such as that inspired by *The Jungle*—over the division of power between democratically elected governments and private interests. The American people—many suffering from the violence inflicted upon them by Pinkerton and other private police forces—fought for the right to organize and to be paid a livable wage. And the American people won. We now have solid worker rights, safer workplaces, and a strong middle class. The American people fought for strong environmental laws against powerful American industrialists who wanted no part of government regulation. And the American people won. Just look at Lake Erie and the Chesapeake Bay and the beaches of California—which were brought back to life—to see how far we have come.

Americans are beginning to understand that the rules of international trade are fundamentally un-American and antidemocratic. NAFTA, the World Trade Organization, and almost every single trade agreement in front of the U.S. Congress shifts power dramatically from elected governments to private interests. One WTO bureaucrat told the *Financial Times,* "The World Trade Organization is the place where governments collude in private against their domestic pressure groups." And former director-general of the World Trade Organization Renato said, "Environmental standards could only damage the global trading system."

In the 1950s fishermen in the eastern Pacific Ocean developed a new way to catch tuna: encirclement nets. In the process of trapping large schools of tuna with these nets, they drowned large numbers of dolphins, which congregate with tuna schools. After these practices killed some seven million dolphins in mostly international waters, Congress passed the Marine Mammal Protection Act, eliminating the most deadly tuna-fishing practices and saving large numbers of dolphins. To further protect tuna, Congress then passed a ban on the importation of tuna that did not meet dolphin conservation standards. In 1990 Congress created the "dolphin safe" labeling program, which became immensely popular with the tuna-buying public, and outlawed the use of that label for tuna caught using the encirclement nets that still killed significant numbers of dolphins. Two years later, Congress banned the sale of all tuna that was not "dolphin safe."

Mexico—home to a major tuna industry—challenged the ban as an unfair trade practice. GATT, the precursor to the World Trade Organization, ruled that U.S. law violated GATT rules and could not exclude products based on how they were produced or harvested. Initially resistant to the ruling, the United States government finally—after the establishment of the World Trade Organization in 1995—realized that it would have to change its law to comply with the international ruling. As the Mexican government threatened action, the United States government was faced with the precedent of a 1998 WTO ruling on an endangered species case: "While the WTO Preamble confirms that environmental considerations are important for the interpretation of the WTO agreement, the central focus of that agreement remains the promotion of economic development through trade; and the provisions of GATT are essentially turned toward liberalization of access to markets on a non-discriminatory basis."

The Clinton administration, now boxed in—not wanting to offend either the fishermen in Mexico or environmentalists in this country, and understanding that retaliatory tariffs might be in the offing—succeeded in changing U.S. law; Mexican fishermen would again be able to sell in the United States tuna caught with encirclement nets, but the "dolphin safe" label could not be affixed to the can. Then the labeling standard passed by Newt Gingrich and a Republican Congress was weakened further. On New Year's Eve 2002, assured that no one was paying attention, President Bush's Commerce secretary Donald Evans quietly announced a weakening of the labeling requirements for "safe dolphins." Public Citizen's Lori Wallach pronounced, "Calling tuna caught using mile-long encirclement nets 'dolphin safe' is a consumer fraud and that fraud has been brought to you by global trade rules under which the United States was instructed to weaken its law." The WTO would simply not let the United States do the right thing for the environment.

Countries with strong environmental, food safety, and consumer protection standards are having great difficulty upholding their laws against hostile corporations or governments that want to sell their products into those countries. For example, in 1997, the United States government, acting on behalf of the American Cattlemen's Association, sued the European Union for unfair trade practices, accusing the Europeans of trying to unfairly protect their own cattle industry. In response to concerns raised by consumers and European public health officials and scientists, the EU had banned the sale of meat which contained bovine growth hormone, a chemical made by Monsanto to increase the size and weight of beef cattle, thus assuring more profitable beef sales for the cattlemen. The WTO trade panel sided with the United States and against the public health law passed by a democratically elected European Union parliament.

The real danger to democracy is the power that these corporations—Monsanto in this case, other multinationals in others—are usurping. Companies frequently convince their pliant governments, even in democracies, to appear on their behalf in front of the World Trade Organization to ask that body to override another country's environmental or food safety law or regulation. There is no accountability when these companies—quietly and effectively—convince their governments to challenge the consumer protection laws of another nation, calling even the existence of such laws unfair trade practices.

U.S. trade policy in the last ten years has centered on the developing world. As Alan Tonelson, chief economist with the United States Business and Industry Council Educational Foundation, pointed out, "U.S. trade policy has backed off from efforts to open Japanese markets, and has conspicuously neglected this mission regarding Europe." The pursuit of trade agreements with developing countries—NAFTA, trading privileges with China, the Africa trade bill, the Caribbean Basin Initiative—seemed to be the major foreign policy goal of the first Bush administration and the Clinton administration. They, and especially their allies among America's largest multinational corporations, seemed far more interested in seeking low-cost production in poor countries than in prying open markets in wealthy nations. The second Bush administration—while rejecting engagement with other nations on arms control, the environment, and eliminating land mines—is pushing ahead on agreements with Vietnam and all of Latin America, except Cuba, of course. And President Bush tells us that he needs Fast Track/Trade Promotion Authority to do it.

These agreements have several things in common. They are mostly investment agreements that provide powerful incentives to serve the lucrative U.S. market from abroad. They shift production from the United States to developing countries, as Western companies troll the world looking for low labor costs, weak environmental laws, and unenforced labor rights. They build in no guarantees for labor and the environment among trading nations. The president's plan for Trade Promotion Authority (TPA) continues in that direction.

Many of us in Congress insisted that any TPA granted to the president had to include enforceable labor and environmental standards. We insisted that Chapter 11—the NAFTA provision that allows corporations to sue governments in other countries, thus allowing a foreign corporation to have more legal authority than a domestic one—be removed. We insisted that Congress reassert itself in trade policy, using our jurisdictional expertise and oversight roles to shine a light on prospective trade agreements. And we insisted on preauthorization so that Congress and the American public would see what is in a trade agreement before it is signed and sent to the House of Representatives and the Senate.

We had seen what could happen even to a relatively good trade agreement. After he had publicly endorsed labor and environmental standards, President Clinton negotiated the Jordan Free Trade Agreement, which included stronger labor and environmental language than any previous trade agreement that the office of the U.S. trade representative had signed. Interestingly, the fine print in the U.S.-Jordan agreement illustrates why Congress must strengthen its ability to review future trade agreements: the U.S. pharmaceutical industry had language inserted in the agreement that provided intellectual property protections more favorable to the drug industry than did even the language governing the World Trade Organization. The Jordan agreement not only imposes barriers to generic drug access in Jordan, it prevents either the United States or Jordan from employing compulsory licensing—a mechanism used by dozens of countries in the world—to rein in inflated drug prices. Stunningly, a relatively minor trade agreement that the United States signed with a country of five million people may prohibit the United States Congress from passing legislation that would help America's senior citizens deal with the oppressively high cost of their prescription drugs.

On the lapel of my jacket, I always wear a small pin depicting a canary in a cage. The canary represents the struggle for economic and social justice in our nation. In the early days of the twentieth century, more than 2,000 American workers were killed in coal mines every year. Miners took a canary into the mines to warn them of toxic gases; if the canary died, they knew they had to escape quickly. Miners were forced to provide for their own protection. No mine safety laws. No trade unions able to help. No real support from their government. A baby born in 1900 had a life expectancy of forty-seven years. Today, thanks to progressive government and an aggressive labor move-ment. Americans can expect to live three decades longer.

It has been a one-hundred-year battle between the privileged and the rest of us. We took on oil and chemical companies to enact clean air and safe drinking water laws. We overcame industry opposition to pass auto safety rules. We beat back insurance and medical interests to establish Medicare and Medicaid for senior citizens and poor chil-dren. We fought off Wall Street bankers to create Social Security. We battled entrenched business interests to enact women's and civil rights, protections for the disabled, and prohibitions on child labor. We fought for all of it.

Every bit of progress made in the struggle for economic and social justice came over the opposition of society's most privileged and most powerful. Remarkably, it was ordinary working families who won so many of these battles against the most entrenched, well-heeled interests. The canary signifies that the struggle continues today, and that all of us must be ever vigilant against the powerful in-terest groups which too often control our government.

4

Myth 4: Free Trade Leaves Most People Better Off—In Rich and Poor Nations Alike

Almost everything we buy, after all, is the product of some other person's suffering and miserably underpaid labor.

—*Barbara Ehrenreich*

It only seems logical. If young girls in Indonesia are paid only a couple of dollars a day to stitch Nike sneakers, then the price of shoes in Lorain, Ohio, will of course go down. If farmers in Mexico earn only about forty dollars a week, then imported tomatoes in Dayton will surely be cheaper. If Disney workers in Bangladesh make only pennies an hour, the price of Disney toys and clothes will certainly be affordable to almost anyone in Akron.

Many free traders claim that global free trade brings great benefits to the world's consumers, especially in the West. Low-cost production (read "cheap labor and nonexistent labor and environmental standards") means, they tell us, less expensive imported products. American consumers surely are more interested in buying at the lowest prices, regardless of where and by whom those products are made.

Everyday, just before sunrise, Cristina Sanchez joins dozens of other young women as they pile into a bright yellow school bus with the words Kent (Ohio) City School District emblazoned on the side. (School buses deemed no longer safe for American children are routinely sold to companies doing business in Latin America.) The destination of this bus is not an Ohio high school but a textile factory in Nicaragua with tight security and surveillance cameras. Here, Cristina joins 26,000 other workers in the Nicaraguan Free Trade Zone, a beehive of foreign-owned factories where mostly young women work about 65 hours a week for 30 to 40 cents an hour.

The companies operating in this free trade zone outside Managua reap exorbitant profits by selling their products in the North American market. The workers at Chentex, a Taiwanese-owned factory in the free trade zone, are paid 21 cents for every pair of jeans they produce. Americans purchase them for $25 at Kohl's and Wal-Mart, which buy them from Chentex for about $7, a markup of more than 300 percent. The wages of the Nicaraguan workers are less than 1 percent of the retail price.

In May 2000, the union representing Chentex workers asked the company for a raise of 13 cents for each pair of jeans sewn. The company refused to negotiate. When the union announced a one-hour work stoppage, the company fired all eleven members of the union's executive board, erected barbed wire on top of the walls surrounding the factory compound, brought in armed guards, and promised to break the union. Within a month, more than 300 workers had lost their jobs and the company had filed a criminal suit against the union leaders. Some of them were reinstated after a subsequent lawsuit and intervention from the U.S. Department of Labor and my office.

Two months later, I visited the crowded, rundown *colonia* of Tipitapa. A suburb ten kilometers outside Managua, Tipitapa is home to

100,000 generally destitute people. It is not hard to tell which companies they work for, because their roofs and walls are constructed or patched with packing materials from the factories. Almost half of the workers in the free trade zone live here. Twenty-one-year-old Cristina told me her story as she stood in the doorway of her one-room shack, holding her three-year-old daughter Maria. The ends of the little girl's hair were discolored, probably a sign of protein deficiency and malnutrition. Her mother told me that her daughter has occasional seizures and suffers from diarrhea, an especially dangerous illness for an infant in a developing country.

Cristina and her husband both work in the free trade zone. Every day, she gets up at 5:00 A.M., makes breakfast, and gets her daughter ready for the trip to the city. With her husband and daughter, Cristina takes three buses to get to work, where she hands Maria over to her grandmother at the factory gate. At the end of the day, she travels across town to pick up Maria; they return home around 8:30 at night. On Sunday, their only "day off," Cristina works as well, cleaning the shack, washing clothes, and preparing meals.

There was palpable fear in Cristina's eyes as she told me of life inside the factory gates—plant managers yelling and screaming, the beatings, and workers' constant fear of losing their jobs if they were to complain. Many of the workers take Sin Sueño, a kind of NoDoz with Vitamin B, perhaps especially made for workers in Latin American sweatshops. If they refuse to work overtime, they lose the pay they had earned that day.

Cristina's family has little to show for their hard work. Sixty-hour workweeks—for both husband and wife—do not provide the basic necessities of life. Their primitive shack is almost impossible to keep clean; their hard dirt floor turns muddy in the rainy season. The mosquito net that covers their bed is ragged and patched. Preventive health care is an unknown concept. Emergency care is prohibitively expensive. They hope to give their daughter a better life, but there is no such thing as free public education in this Managua barrio.

Families in Tipitapa will likely never know or see a decent standard of living. A new factory in the United States usually means good pay, hundreds of other jobs in the neighborhood, more money for local school districts, and an increased standard of living for the whole community. But in developing countries, foreign investors pay workers so little that the workers share in almost none of the wealth they create. Cristina will never buy the jeans she makes. And few foreign companies pay taxes to the community in which they are located—for schools, health clinics, or sewer systems. To Cristina, her husband, and their daughter, the free trade zone barely keeps them alive.

Free traders argue that American consumers enjoy significantly lower prices because of more cheaply produced goods imported under lower tariffs. Although the United States has lowered tariffs under NAFTA and WHO, and thousands of factories have relocated overseas, there is no evidence that companies that invest in manufacturing facilities overseas pass along appreciable cost savings to American consumers. When Nike moved all of its production overseas, the price of its shoes did not decrease. Clothes made for Disney for only a few cents an hour in Bangladesh are still expensive in the United States. Tomatoes grown in Mexico after the enactment of NAFTA actually cost more in the United States than those grown in Florida before NAFTA. American farmers lost their jobs, and American consumers paid 16 percent higher prices for tomatoes, according to U.S. government statistics. And while Chentex workers receive 21 cents for each pair of jeans they sew, and the Taiwanese company sells the jeans to American retailers for seven dollars, Kohl's 300 percent markup means that American consumers are not benefiting from the low-wage Nicaraguan workers' sacrifice.

To be sure, the world's largest corporations benefit from the unrestricted global commerce that we call free trade. Transnational corporations account for more than one-third of global output; their global annual sales have reached well over five trillion dollars. Of the one hundred largest economies in the world, fifty-one are corporations. The largest one hundred multinational corporations control about one-third of all foreign direct investment. And the rich are getting phenomenally richer. R.C. Longworth pointed out in the *Chicago Tribune* in July 1999, that the three richest officers of Microsoft—Bill Gates, Paul Allen, and Steve Ballmer—had more assets (nearly $140 billion) than the combined gross national product of the forty-three least-developed countries in the world; 600 million people reside in those forty-three countries. In 1960 the richest fifth of the world's people had thirty times as much income as the poorest fifth. Today, that portion has almost tripled, to more than 80–1: while the fifth of the world's people living in the richest countries collected 86 percent of the world's income, the fifth in the poorest accounted for only a minuscule 1 percent. The United Nations Development Program's annual global review, the *Human Development Report*, stated in July 1999, "When the market goes too far in dominating social and political outcomes, the opportunities and rewards of globalization spread unequally and inequitably—concentrating power and wealth in a select group of people, nations, and corporations, marginalizing the others."

Most developing countries, especially those that are not democracies, have never developed large middle classes. Typically, with some notable exceptions such as India, they have no real democratic structure that can lead to a building-up of a middle class. A small number of people controls investment, business, the media, the government, and major portions of the country's natural and economic resources. It is they and their agents who bring in the investment, recruit the labor, and facilitate the production coming from the West to their countries. As the poor and working class in industrial democracies bear the brunt of free trade, it is the rich in the less-developed nations—and the rich in the wealthy nations—who are the beneficiaries.

The UNDP's *Human Development Report* stated, "Global inequalities in income and living standards have reached grotesque proportions. . . . The privatization and concentration of technology are going too far. Corporations define research agendas. . . . Money talks, not need. Cosmetic drugs and slow-ripening tomatoes come higher on the priority list than drought-resistant crops or a vaccine against malaria." Journalist Ken Silverstein noted that the French scientific journal *Cahiers Sante* found in 1996 that of forty-one important medicines used to treat major tropical diseases, none was discovered in the 1990s and all but six were discovered before 1985. And while more than six million people in the developing world die each year of tuberculosis, acute lower respiratory infections, or malaria, only 1 percent of new medicines brought to market by the world's largest pharmaceutical companies in the last twenty years were designed specifically to treat tropical diseases.

Global economic growth has failed to generate prosperity for the masses. Only thirty-three countries managed to sustain a 3 percent annual gross domestic product growth on a per capita basis between 1980 and 1996; in many of those countries the growth in wealth was very unevenly distributed. In fifty-nine countries, there was no growth at all; per capita GDP actually declined. Eighty countries have lower per capita incomes today than they did a decade ago. Half the world's people are living—if you can call it that—on less than $2 a day. The World Bank reported that 200 million more people today are living in desperate poverty—on less than one dollar a day!—than in 1987. As Jay Mazur, president of the Union of Needletrades, Industrial, and Textile Employees (UNITE), pointed out: "Contrary to popular opinion, those left behind are often the most integrated into global trade. For example, sub-Saharan Africa has a higher export-to-GDP ratio than Latin America, but its exports are mainly primary commodities, leaving those nations vulnerable to the volatility of those markets. The Africa trade bill—passed by Congress without debt relief provisions or enforcement of labor rights and environmental standards—merely offers old wine in new bottles." Coffee farmers have seen their incomes drop by more than half, victimized by the volatility of prices brought on by the World Bank, the International Monetary Fund, and forces in the global economy over which these farmers have no influence or control.

Over the past two decades, since the days of Margaret Thatcher and Ronald Reagan, the World Bank and the International Monetary Fund, supported and promoted by the United States Department of Treasury, have been, in the words of Canadian writer Linda McQuaig, "remodeling the world along strict market lines"—using their lending power to force poor countries to adopt market reforms. Many of the market reforms we seek abroad, where *corporate* interests control, have been rejected domestically when *democracy* rules: we have, for most of the last century in the United States, strengthened our social safety net, increased worker safety, regulated food safety, incentivized health insurance, enabled fair collective bargaining, cleaned up the environment, and provided a better standard of living for millions of families. Yet on behalf of corporate interests, Western lending institutions—led by the IMF and the World Bank—have pushed privatization and deregulation, the so-called Washington Consensus, on developing nations. They have weakened labor protections and environmental safeguards. They have conditioned laws on slashing education spending and health-care expenditures. They have forced developing nations to move away from sustainable agriculture to commodity exports, such as coffee and chocolate, which are consumed mostly in wealthy nations. The promises sounded good when the experts told these countries how it would work. Farmers could earn more, officials told them, by shifting from subsistence farming to selling coffee or cocoa beans to rich countries. Thousands of Vietnamese farmers, at the strong urging of the World Bank and the International Monetary Fund, abandoned their traditional farming practices and began in the early 1990s to shift rice and other foodstuff production to coffee. Bankers tempted the farmers with carrots and threatened them with sticks, promising a higher standard of living brought on by exports and the hard currency the coffee would bring. The countries that these bankers represented—France, Japan, the United States, Great Britain, Canada, Belgium—had developed their economies very differently; they in fact had protected their industries. But the financial and corporate interests that the IMF and the World Bank represented assured those in the developing world that this sharp change in their economy was medicine that they just had to take.

Vietnam increased its coffee production dramatically. Even though world consumption of coffee continued to rise, the piper eventually would have to be paid, tragically by dirt farmers scratching out a living in dozens of developing countries, not by bankers in the world's cosmopolitan financial centers. As Vietnam moved up from the fifteenth largest coffee grower to second (behind only Brazil), a flooded world market caused prices to plummet. Twenty-five million farmers in Latin America, Asia, and Africa saw prices fall by 70 percent, to about 40 cents per pound. As the prices paid to small farmers dropped, the profits to the huge coffee companies swelled. In Central America, coffee widows—women whose husbands left the coffee farms to seek jobs in the cities (they hoped only temporarily until coffee prices went up)—proliferated. Others sold their small plots of land to big coffee plantations, hoping to find new ways to support their families.

Enter fair trade, a third-party monitoring system called TransFair USA, and millions of coffee drinkers in Europe and North America. Fair trade has enabled small farmers to organize cooperatives, skip the middleman, and sell their coffee—with a "Fair trade" label affixed to it—to coffee importers in the wealthy nations. The Fair Trade label, by agreement with the major coffee wholesalers and retailers, signifies that farmers are paid a floor price of $1.26/pound and that the coffee is grown with environmentally sound practices. "Fair trade," Trans-Fair executive director Paul Rice told me in the coffee highlands north of Managua, "is empowerment that changes people's lives." About 700,000 farmers in twenty-two countries benefit from fair trade coffee. But while the success of fair trade coffee is meaningful, it accounts for only about 5 percent of coffee sales worldwide.

It is possible the situation in developing countries is about to change. Canadian finance minister Paul Martin, chairman of the G20—the group of finance ministers from both the G8 and emerging nations like China and India—worries that the IMF and the World Bank simply are not doing it right. "To go into a country and say, as a condition of getting a loan, you're going to privatize, you're going to reform your pension system . . . and here are another 45 things you're going to do—which no G7 country could do within a short time period, let alone an impoverished country with a very weak public service—it's just unrealistic and unacceptable. And yet this kind of thing goes on all the time."

The collapse of the fifth WTO ministerial in Cancún in September 2003 gave new hope to developing-world farmers. The proposed draft ministerial texts thrust onto the agenda by the richest countries would have done little to reduce the advantages that Western agriculture subsidies have provided for the largest agribusiness concerns in the country.

Even in the United States, the wealth generated by free trade has made little difference among large segments of the population. Trade is almost twice as large a part of GDP today as it was in 1973, when the U.S. trade surplus turned—apparently permanently—to a deficit. The median real wage—the level at which 50 percent of the country's wage earners are above and 50 percent of the country's wage earners are below—in the United States has been stagnant over the last twenty-seven years. Compare that stagnation of wages among half the population with the period from 1946–1973, when the average U.S. wage increased by 80 percent.

There is a heavy price for society to pay when workers and communities lose good-paying industrial jobs. People are not just consumers, but workers who pay taxes. Every pair of New Balance running shoes made in Massachusetts results in U.S. workers paying into Social Security and Medicare, and funding public schools, public highways, and public safety. If people who manufacture shoes in the United States lose their jobs and take lower-paying jobs, they are often unable to afford the cost of other products. Tax rates may go up as tax bases erode and local governments' tax revenues decline, and as people lose jobs and end up unemployed or working in lower-paid jobs, society obviously pays a price in social costs—crime, alcoholism, divorce, and everything else that comes with sudden personal, economic upheaval.

The announcement came as a shock to 6,500 mostly Mexican-American women. They had worked hard. They were productive. They played by the rules. Now they had lost their jobs in Levi Strauss plants in Texas, Colorado, and California. They had not seen it coming. Only six months earlier, they had watched Thomas Tusher, the second top executive at this 146-year-old family-owned company, walk away with a golden parachute of $127 million. It was originally planned to be $100 million, but the company threw in the rest to offset his taxes. One of the laid-off workers in the plant in Laredo calculated that if the 6,500 workers had split the retirement package awarded to Tusher, each of them would have received about $18,000, more than a year's pay for these slightly-above-minimum-wage workers. Then, 18 months later, Levi Strauss dropped the other shoe. On George Washington's birthday in 1999, this emblem of American popular culture announced that it was closing half its plants in the United States and Canada. Another 5,500 employees, 30 percent of its North American workforce, would lose their jobs. Ten plants in the United States would shut down, and one in Ontario, Canada, would cease production. Management usually referred to these job losses as a "necessary restructuring" of its company in response to the highly competitive global economy. By 2001, some corporate public relations officials spoke of the "global rebalancing" necessary in today's economy.

To its credit, Levi Strauss did reasonably well for its employees, offering a package of benefits worth about $245 million, including eight months' notice, three weeks of severance pay for every year of service to the company, enhanced early retirement benefits, extended medical coverage, and an allowance of up to $6,000 to pay for education or retraining costs.

The plant closings in 1997 were, according to company management, a response to Levi's problems of excess capacity. The announcement of the eleven plant closings in 1999 signaled a shift in production to Mexico and other developing countries with significantly less expensive labor and an outsourcing whereby Levi Strauss would begin to use private contractors in seventy countries to manu-facture their jeans. The average labor costs, including benefits, of $10.12 an hour in the U.S. garment industry were just too much in the face of wages in Mexico and other Latin American nations.

While appreciative of the settlement by the company, Bruce Raynor, the secretary-treasurer of UNITE, blamed the direction of the industry on the North American Free Trade Agreement. He pointed out that Levi Strauss was one of the last holdouts that still did manufacturing in the United States. In the manufacturers' "race to the bottom," workers all over the world lose, as companies—some by choice, others, like Levi Strauss, to compete with those which al-ready have made the move—shut their productive facilities and move elsewhere.

Five years later, in April 2002, the 149-year-old company an-nounced that it would close six more of its plants, leaving only one U.S. manufacturing operation. In late 2003 Levi Strauss closed its last U.S. plant. In fact, the company makes no jeans anywhere in the world; all their production is subcontracted.

In this inexorable race to the bottom, transnational corporations seem to be getting their way. Inadequate wages, environmental dam-age, and unregulated capital are conspiring against people in rich and poor countries alike. A larger company purchases a large company, a few executives take out millions of dollars in bonuses, stock options, and golden parachutes, and several thousand workers lose their jobs. And transnational corporate profits soar.

Along the United States–Mexico border in the *maquiladoras* are 3,000 industrial plants employing about one million workers. The plants are almost all less than 15 years old, and most contain state-of-the-art technology. They pay little or no property taxes. The workers are the most productive in Mexico, and some of the most productive in the world. Most earn not much more than a dollar an hour. None belongs to an independent trade union, yet their employers have *their* cartel. Employers convene in each region of the *maquiladoras* about once every month—to discuss benefits, to work out problems, and to set wages. After one meeting, for example, in late November 1998, they announced their agreement—not with the workers but among the employers—to increase wages for *maquiladora* workers 14 percent, notably less than the inflation rate of 18 percent. Worker productivity that year had increased, yet wages in real purchasing power went down. The employers met again in 1999 and again in late 2000 to set wages. University of California at Berkeley economist Harley Shaiken said, "The irony is, with all the talk about free trade, we have highly controlled labor markets when it comes to wage setting. When you combine Mexican government policy, weak union or government-controlled unions, and employers who are collaborating in these areas, what you get are very low wages in combination with high productivity." Mexican wages, Shaikin told me one day in December 2003, are "anchored to the bottom." If they weren't, *maquiladora* officials—American or Mexican—would argue, competing for workers would cause a very damaging spiraling of out-of-control wages.

The *maquiladoras* are the crown jewel of the Mexican economy. They attract hundreds of billions of dollars in foreign investment, principally from the United States but also from East Asia and Europe. These companies, which the Mexican government believes are the engine of the Mexican economy, bring in billions of dollars from exports, help Mexico pay its debts, and make Mexico an especially attractive place for investors.

However, the Mexican government understands that these factory owners have no more loyalty to Mexico and to the *maquiladoras* than they did to the United States and the American community in which they were located before. They know that the fast-paced and largely unregulated movement of capital victimizes developing countries. Factories and communities are abandoned as capital flees to more profitable pastures. International financier George Soros worries about the invisible hand with no democratic controls. He wrote in *Foreign Policy* in late 1998 that "financial markets are inherently unstable and always will be. . . . The very notion of equilibrium is false." Earlier that year he told a gathering of free traders at the World Economic Forum in Davos, Switzerland, as reported by *Harper's* magazine's Lewis Lapham, that only fools believed in the conscience of markets—fools and tenured professors of economics. Markets were as dumb as posts and as blind as bats, inherently unstable because they are dependent upon what people wish for, not what they have in hand. "Financial markets are given to excesses," he said, "and when a boom/bust sequence progresses beyond a certain point, it inevitably transforms the economic fundamental, which in turn can never revert to where they began."

On a global scale the invisible hand can be more dangerous, Soros told the Davos gathering, who were admirers of his success but increasingly uneasy with his message. "Imagine a pendulum that has become a wrecking ball, swinging out of control and with increasing speed, knocking over one economy after another. First Mexico, then Indonesia and South Korea, and who knows what happens next?"

Deregulated Asian economies were set upon by "hedge funds," huge conglomerations of wealth from Western investors. Most Western bankers and financial analysts, highly critical of Asian banks for their secrecy and lack of transparency, saw nothing wrong with the total opaqueness under which long-term capital management and other hedge funds operated. Thailand, Indonesia, and Malaysia were generally unprotected because, in part, they had followed Western advice, the kind of direction that the International Monetary Fund and the World Bank had been giving for years: Restrict domestic demand so that currency can be stabilized and foreign debts can be paid. Raise interest rates, cut government spending, increase taxes. Shred the expensive safety net, weaken unions and the wage pressures that they bring, and cut spending on education and infrastructure. Most important, bring in financiers to deregulate securities and banks and then install those financiers to run what's left of the regulatory system. Make it easier to move foreign capital in and out of the country.

To the IMF, which, in Harvard economist Jeffrey Sachs's words, "believes in a single cause of macroeconomic disease: excessive budget deficits," the cure for a collapsing economy is always the same—cut the budget and raise interest rates to encourage foreign investors to hold onto the domestic currency. A country that must follow IMF advice to defend its currency and its exchange rate at any cost is a country that must become an export economy to pay back its very oppressive debts. Few countries ever can.

"Things and money," said Brazilian professor Roberto Ungar, "are free to roam the world, yet labor is locked into its own country; it's called economic freedom." Financial capital obeys basic laws of capitalism and economics. It naturally flows to its most advantageous and profitable use. Logically, capital goes to the countries and economies where it has the freest reign, where it is most unfettered, where government leaves it mostly unregulated. Labor, on the other hand, is immobile, especially in totalitarian countries and less developed nations, and capital typically lands in those economies where labor costs are lowest and labor itself is the most immobile. Fast-moving, unregulated capital creates instability.

David Ranson and Penny Russell, two free traders writing in the *Wall Street Journal,* described unregulated capital—approvingly— this way:

The owners of capital are constantly on the lookout for the most profitable—and safe—way to use it. When a country engages in policies that hinder or jeopardize profitable use of capital, that economy is "punished" for such behavior when the capital flees. The owners of that capital . . . will put it to work in an economy . . . that provides an . . . unburdensome environment for economic effort.

They envision an ideal world as a place where "capital can freely migrate to where it can realize the best return and in which the punishment of unfriendly policies is swift." Unfriendly policies, it is assumed, are labor standards, environmental regulations, and the health and safety consensus to which most Americans have ascribed.

Mexican senator Amalia Garcia believes capital flight—which she likens to a *golondrina*, a Mexican swallow "that always flies about"—is the single most serious problem facing developing countries' economic growth. She understands that capital is free to "fly about," but she is anxious to somehow rein it in, perhaps with better data, some financial regulation, taxation, and more democratic oversight.

But that is likely not good enough. *Harper's* editor Lewis Lapham wrote of a 1998 conference in New York City at which many of America's most prominent financiers and corporate leaders were lamenting the poor market supervision of Asian financial markets:

Laura Tyson, the former chair of President Clinton's Council of Economic Advisers, interrupted the discussion to observe that the heavy capital flows that had drowned the Asian economies didn't come from Asia. They came from Europe and the United States, from fully developed industrial countries well equipped with sufficient data and the instruments of democratic oversight. What we are talking about here, she said, is greed . . . stupidity, cowardice, and greed . . . about investors in London and Paris and New York seizing the prey of easy profits and then, when the luck went bad, seeking to transfer their losses to a government . . . about privatizing the gains, socializing the losses.

Developing nations are at a great disadvantage in other ways as well. Dr. Robert Aboagye-Mensah, the general secretary of the Christian Council of Ghana, said, "International trade between my country and the West is like an antelope and a giraffe competing for food which is at the top of a tree. You can make the ground beneath their feet level, but the contest will still not be fair." When sophisticated, wealthy, transnational corporations collide with the tradition, communal interests, and culture of a developing nation, the poorer nation is always overmatched. In rural, less developed, traditional societies, writes Indian author Vandana Shiva, "biodiversity is common property, and knowledge related to it is in the intellectual commons. For biotechnology corporations, biodiversity becomes private property through their investments, and intellectual property rights are the means for such privatization."

Peasant farmers in developing countries who have experimented with cross-breeding, hybrids, and seed variations on their farms and in their villages for centuries have no protection from large Western biotech firms that claim intellectual property rights as their own. In early 1993, anticipating what was about to happen to them and their way of life, 250,000 Indian farmers rallied at Delhi's Red Fort to protest the Uruguay round of the General Agreement on Tariffs and Trade. Their organizers proclaimed that:

> Our genetic resources are our national property. We oppose patents or any form of intellectual property protection on

plants and genes. To produce, modify, and sell seeds is the right of the farmers. We want a ban on the entry of Multi-National Corporations in the seed sector. We want the preservation of the Indian Patent Act of 1970 which excludes patents on all life forms.

Historically, Indian patent law protected agricultural and biodiversity, allowing no intellectual property claims on that which has been developed communally over generations. Article 3(h) of the Indian Patent Law of 1970 specifies that, "patents cannot be given for a method of agriculture or horticulture." Article 3(i) states that "patents cannot be given for any process for the medicinal, surgical, curative, prophylactic or other treatment of human beings or any process for a similar treatment of animals or plants to render them free of disease or to increase their economic value." Shiva, director of the Research Foundation for Science, Technology and Natural Resource Policy in Dehradun, India, wrote, "These exclusions of the Indian Patent Act that have kept agriculture out of the monopoly control of the corporate sector are now threatened."

Indian Patent law directly collides with GATT, Article 27 of the Trade-Related Intellectual Property Rights (TRIP), which unequivocally orders: "Patents shall be available for any invention, whether products or processes." And Western biotech firms, armed with Article 27, will demand that their firms be allowed to enter India, and that they enjoy the intellectual property rights to which they are now legally entitled. One Western agribusiness executive intoned, "Even though it has been a tradition in most countries that a farmer can save seed from his own crop, it is, under the changing circumstances, not equitable that a farmer can use this seed and grow a commercial crop out of it without a payment of royalty. The seed industry will have to fight harder for a better kind of protection."

This privatization of community assets, in some ways not much different from efforts by some in Congress to privatize Medicare and our national park system, is all too tempting for Western agribusiness, biotech, and pharmaceutical firms. The objective of these firms is not difficult to understand. Through assertion of their newly acquired property rights bestowed on them by GATT and other international trade agreements, they want to expand their markets by monopolizing the seed supply, and force farmers to buy their seed every year. And these huge, Western companies want tradition, communal knowledge, and small farmers out of their way. John Hamilton of Cargill India, one of the world's largest grain companies, lauded his company's technology for making hybrid sunflowers because they prevent "bees from usurping the pollen."

Investors might love the sudden rise in short-term profits, and stocks might rally on reports of downsizing and outsourcing, but long-term growth prospects for U.S. companies suffer when low-wage countries delay the development of vibrant middle classes that can afford the high-value products for which the United States is well known. As long as wages stay low in developing countries, workers will never be able to buy what they make, and global supply will continue to outrun global demand. As long as workers in developing countries are paid less than the value they add to a product, worldwide demand will continue to stagnate. These workers add to the global supply of goods, they add significant value to the products they assemble, yet they are unable to purchase the goods they make or share in the wealth they create. And the results will be that workers in poor countries will stay poor, and they will drag down the wages in wealthy countries.

Roughly the same challenge faces U.S. policy makers. In industry after industry there is a surplus of capacity and a lack of demand. The only solution is to create new markets, just as Henry Ford did in the early years of industrial America. Unfortunately, our policies of the last thirty years have been more successful at creating trade deficits than new markets. Western businessmen who talk of new markets, almost breathlessly citing one billion Chinese consumers, for example, are far more interested in one billion Chinese as potential workers. Goods shipped from the United States to China for assembly and reexport increased 349 percent in the five years leading up to the 2000 establishment of Permanent Normal Trade Relations with China. Agreements such as NAFTA and GATT have helped balloon our merchandise trade deficit beyond $200 billion precisely because they have been investor-oriented rather than market-oriented. For all the talk about opening foreign markets to U.S. goods, the main impact of recent U.S. trade policy has been to protect American investors from the risk of expropriation, or to facilitate American investors' use of low-wage foreign export platforms.

In the long run, such a shortsighted policy can only prove harmful to American companies and American workers. While NAFTA or GATT may lower the risk for investors, these trade agreements undermine the process of creating new markets for American products. Producing in low-wage dictatorships and selling to high-wage democracies make sense for the transnational corporation and for the dictator but not for workers in either group of countries and not for the poor and the middle class anywhere.

Not even the investors themselves benefit in the long run. The contradictions will surely come home to roost. U.S. workers see their wages stagnate due to increased competition from low-wage countries such as Indonesia and Malaysia and China, whose authoritarian governments prevent their workers from winning pay raises through the process of democracy and collective bargaining. As their wages stagnate, their purchasing power erodes, and the market shrinks. When a seventeen-year-old $3-a-day Indonesian worker displaces a

Massachusetts union shoemaker, it means there is one fewer consumer who can buy shoes, or a car, or a television.

Some companies never stop trying. On January 13, 1999, several lawsuits were filed against U.S. retailers and manufacturers accusing them of engaging in a "racketeering conspiracy" to produce apparel in sweatshop conditions, in slave labor conditions, on a U.S. island territory. Eighteen U.S. companies—including such giants as WalMart, Sears, The Gap, Tommy Hilfiger, Nordstrom, The Limited, J.C. Penney, and Lord and Taylor's—were named. Twenty-two factories on the island of Saipan, located in the Commonwealth of Northern Mariana Islands (CNMI), were charged with violations of U.S. law.

CNMI, made up of fourteen islands and located in the South Pacific closer to the Philippines than to Hawaii, is a U.S. territory. Liberated from Japan at the end of the Second World War, and then annexed to the United States, the islands are home to about 60,000 people and attract thousands of Japanese tourists. Thanks to its effective lobbying efforts and its political obscurity, it has been allowed to operate outside U.S. labor law—with lower minimum wages and less strict environmental and worker safety laws—while still affixing the "Made in USA" label that makes products more attractive in U.S. retail outlets. Companies on the islands can employ foreign workers, most of them young women from China, Bangladesh, Thailand, and the Philippines, who work for only a few cents an hour.

Some 40,000 workers sew a billion dollars' worth of apparel annually for huge U.S. retailers. Many workers have paid recruitment fees of as much as $7,000 that traps them in indentured servitude. According to Larry Weiss of the Minnesota Fair Trade Coalition and U.S. government statistics, workers face workweeks of up to eighty-four hours with overtime hours often uncompensated and obligatory contracts that waive basic human rights, including the freedom to join unions, attend religious services, quit their jobs, or marry.

Corporations in the Northern Marianas and the island government itself put together, in anticipation of congressional opposition to their practices, a sophisticated lobbying campaign so that they could continue to enjoy its special status. From hiring expensive and well-connected Washington lobbyists to arranging expensive and frequent junkets for Texas congressman Tom DeLay and other members of the Republican leadership, the Northern Mariana Islands coalition was successful in preserving what it had.

Filed by Asian workers, American trade unions, and international human rights groups, the lawsuits claim that thousands of Asians were brought to the island with unfulfilled promises of good wages; once there, many were beaten, some were forced to get abortions, and all were required to live under guard in rat-infested barracks. Most of the American companies named in the suit said they hire South Korean and Chinese subcontractors who are instructed to follow U.S. labor law. It was a common practice in the 1990s—and still is—for large American corporations, which have assiduously cultivated their images and have prestigious names, to contract with local companies that then hire child labor, pay little heed to worker rights, and ignore any environmental safeguards that a country might impose. If they are caught, as Nike was in Indonesia and these giant retailers have been in Saipan, they can plead ignorance and feign righteousness.

California Democratic congressman George Miller introduced legislation first in 1997, then in subsequent years, to apply labor and immigration standards to the CNMI and its products. But the government of the Northern Mariana Islands and the corporations and investors on the islands were ready. They unleashed a $2,000,000 lobbying campaign, retaining former Republican presidential candidate Bob Dole's Washington, D.C.–based firm Verner, Liipfert, Bernhard,

McPherson and Hand. They entertained dozens of congressional staffers, inviting key legislative aides to come see for themselves. And come they did to this beautiful tropical island paradise; thirteen trips including six members of Congress and sixty-five House and Senate aides in 1997 alone—at a cost of about $6,000 each. Republican leadership was especially well-represented on perhaps the most sought-after junkets of the year, as top aides to then–Majority Leader Dick Armey and Majority Whip Tom DeLay visited. Republican leadership has scheduled no hearings on Miller's bill. The island continues to receive federal largesse, more than $85 million every year.

With only 4 percent of the world's population living in the United States, and only another 10 percent living in Canada, Western Europe, Australia, and Japan, who will purchase the goods made by the hundreds of millions of men and women earning only a few dollars a day? Nike paid more money in 1998 to Michael Jordan than it paid its entire 30,000 Vietnamese workforce of mostly young village girls. Who will buy the shoes? General Motors, Mexico's largest private employer, pays its workers about fifty dollars a week. Who will buy the cars? Young Bangladeshi women earn less than subsistence wages in textile plants for Disney. Who will buy the toys? Malaysian workers earn three dollars a day working for Motorola. Who will buy the cell phones? Nicaraguan workers earn 21 cents for each pair of pants they sew. Who will buy the jeans?

In 1960, before globalization, the most affluent 20 percent of the world's population was thirty times richer than the poorest 20 percent. By 1997, the most fortunate were seventy-four times richer than the world's poorest. And the chasm is widening. The combined fortunes of the 400 richest people in the world equals more than the annual income of the poorest 50 percent of the world's people. The sad reality is that there is no real mechanism in our trade laws to help the developing countries share the wealth that is being generated by trade. Nevertheless, those who represent global investors such as the World Bank and the International Monetary Fund continue to insist that developing countries balance their budgets and cut spending, especially on education and public infrastructure, to make global investment more attractive. As they celebrate the "victory" of the free market, they purposely ignore the lessons that they themselves learned so many years ago—that public spending, building local industry and infrastructure, and democracy must go hand in hand to build a middle class and a prosperous nation.

Behind their celebration of free, unregulated markets is all too often contempt for political democracy. Investors do best, at least in the short run and at least in their own minds, when capital is free and unregulated. They want capital to be free to perform without health and safety regulations, without labor standards, and without constraint. But in the long run, the issue is not so clear. Without democratic controls, neither investors nor the public is protected. Kuttner wrote, "We need the habits and institutions of a strong democracy precisely to keep markets in their place and to provide resilience during those historical periods when the market goes haywire and makes ordinary people vulnerable to the appeals of tyrants."

Yet global investors continue to chase after authoritarian governments that are very hospitable to their investments and where workers are compliant. According to a November 1999 report issued by the New Economy Information Service, the share of developing-country exports to the United States represented by developing democracies fell from 53.4 percent in 1989 to 34.9 percent in 1998, a decrease of 18.5 percentage points. In manufactured goods, developing democracies' share of developing-country exports fell 21.6 percentage points, from 56.7 percent to 35.1 percent. Corporations are relocating their manufacturing bases to more authoritarian regimes, where the workers do not talk back for fear of being punished. As developing nations make progress toward democracy, as they increase worker rights and create regulations to protect the environment, the American business community punishes them by pulling its trade and investment in favor of more totalitarian governments.

The UNDP's *Human Development Report* warned the world's leaders: "The challenge is not to stop the expansion of global markets. The challenge is to find the rules and institutions for stronger governance . . . to preserve the advantage of global markets and competition but also to provide enough space for human, community, and environmental resources to ensure that globalization works for people, not just for profits."

Successive U.S. administrations have pressured other countries to adopt the Washington Consensus and accept our ideas on intellectual property rights, the deregulation of financial markets, and the privatization of state-run services. Using our wealth, our very attractive market, and our political power, we have required poor countries to remake their economies, enriching American investors and multinational corporations and establishing programs in poorer nations to assist their development on our terms. The Structural Adjustment Programs (SAPs) administered by the World Bank and the International Monetary Fund take developing economies in exactly the opposite direction from that in which successful economies have gone. They stabilize currency so debts to Western nations and Western banks can be paid; slash government spending, especially on health care and education; raise interest rates so that foreign investors will keep their domestic currency; increase taxes; and deregulate securities—all in the name of building an export economy.

Those countries that followed another course—the nations of

Western Europe and the United States in the eighteenth century, and Japan and the four "Asian Tigers" in the twentieth century—obviously did much better. They used high levels of protective trade barriers and tariffs. They heavily subsidized their domestic industry. They invested in education, protected their markets, redistributed land, set tariffs and subsidized their exports, and ran trade surpluses. The governments in these now-developed nations gave strong support for state-owned industries. Yet we tell Mexico, Indonesia, and other poor nations to privatize and sell off government and societal assets to their own nation's elite or to Western investors. The now-wealthy Western nations once encouraged strong support for economic diversification for themselves but now force on developing economies a small number of export products, citing economists' "comparative advantage" as their theory. While Western nations imposed strong capital and currency controls on themselves, decades later they lowered currency and capital controls in poorer countries. Thus the primary purpose of governments in the developed world seems to be to protect the property rights of corporate investors in the rest of the world.

Taiwan, Singapore, Hong Kong, and South Korea have refused to abide by these requirements and have fared much better. Rick Rowden of the RESULTS Educational Fund described the rapid development of the four "Asian Tiger" nations:

> The Four Tigers model, like the history of European, Japanese, and American models over the last 150 years, strengthens the state; the SAPs model weakens the state.
>
> The Four Tigers model allows the state and domestic industries to be the main beneficiaries; the SAPs model allows for international investors to be the primary beneficiaries.
>
> The Four Tigers model [has competed] with, and in some

sectors out-competes, First World multinational corporations since the late 1970s; the SAPs model complements and privileges First World multinational corporations.

Interestingly, the severe economic problems that the Four Tigers experienced in the late 1990s came about because they succumbed to pressures from Western governments to open up their economies and deregulated their financial and banking systems.

Why do we impose the harsh requirements of our capital markets with none of the counterweights to market forces that wealthy countries enjoy? Why should we not try to sell and promote around the world our whole economic package—a package that includes labor, environment, and human rights? If we protect intellectual property rights, Hollywood movies, patents, and CD-ROMs, why not protect the environment, worker rights, and food safety?

We need to protect basic human rights for workers around the world: freedom from child labor, forced labor, and discrimination; freedom to join together with others in a union to have a voice at work. We are so proud of our success at exporting our products around the world; we must work with equal pride in exporting our democratic values, human rights, labor rights, and environmental standards. After all, a global economy that fails to lift the standard of living and honor the values of working men and women—those who help create the world's wealth—will not work. If it does not work for those who create the world's products and the world's wealth, then it will not work at all.

5

Myth 5: Free Trade Will Bring Democracy, Human Rights, and Freedom to Authoritarian Nations

U.S. companies always look the other way when China breaks the rules. . . . Our greatest adversary on human rights is American business. . . .

—Wei Jingsheng, Chinese human rights activist

They say it over and over. On the House floor. In committee. In our offices. If one theme dominates the trade debate in the United States House of Representatives, it is that the best way to promote democracy around the world is to engage in free trade with totalitarian countries, especially the People's Republic of China (PRC).

Free trade, they tell us, will bring free markets, and with free markets will come political freedom. That policy of "constructive engagement" with China has consistently carried the day in Congress. The immense amount of American investment in China, the wealth it is providing that country, and the exposure to Western culture and values that it brings to the people are turning the Chinese away from communist totalitarianism, or so the American public is told.

Newspaper publishers, conservative politicians, and business leaders who worship at the altar of free trade continue to insist that unregulated global capitalism leads inevitably to democracy. They learned it in political science class. They read it in economics textbooks. It will happen, they assure us, in China, Indonesia, and all over the less-developed, totalitarian world. But world history tells us something very different. The rise of twentieth-century Germany and Japan, fueled by industrial capitalism, led to fascism, not democracy. Both countries enjoyed great success in their economies, experiencing tremendous economic growth and rapid industrialization. Business had a free hand and a cooperative government. They built war machines from the profits of their industrial enterprises and the technology that those industries brought them. But there was little political freedom for their citizens.

Business in Chile also had a free hand and a cooperative government. General Augusto Pinochet, with the help of American president Richard Nixon, top foreign policy advisor Henry Kissinger, and the Central Intelligence Agency, had overthrown an elected socialist government with a military coup in 1973 and transformed the economy of Chile. Working hand in hand with the Chicago School of Economics, the Pinochet government moved the country from social democracy to free-market capitalism. But little freedom existed in the society as a whole outside of the marketplace. Wealth created by a capitalist system with little political democracy almost always exacerbates the differences between rich and poor. During Pinochet's reign, wealth increased, Chile's poverty rate remained unchanged, and civil liberties were sharply curtailed.

In Indonesia, "free trade" and rapid industrial growth have failed to move that country toward democracy. For thirty years Indonesia experienced phenomenal growth, but an overwhelming majority of the population is still very poor, and the country, until its devastating economic crisis in 1999, was still controlled by a right-wing military dictatorship with no real prospects for human rights, free labor, or democracy. Human rights abuses, especially in East Timor, have abounded. The government, business, and the military act as one to control the country's wealth and economy. The first seeds of democracy sprouted only when Indonesia's slavish devotion to free-trade policies crashed during the Asian financial crisis.

Latin American dictatorships—usually supported and often sponsored by the United States—have been especially friendly to American business interests. A significant aim of U.S. foreign policy in Latin America in the past century has been to make the region safe and secure for large U.S. businesses. Too often, the United States has been on the wrong side of history in the fight for human rights and democracy around the globe, especially in Latin America. Avowed free trader Rodrik commented, "Latin America, the region that adopted the globalization agenda with the greatest enthusiasm in the 1990s, has suffered rising inequality, enormous volatility, and economic growth rates significantly below those of the post–World War II decades."

Financial interests of U.S. companies—with none more important than the United Fruit Company—almost always drive U.S. foreign policy in Latin America. The term "banana republic" is derived from the policy that propped up Latin American dictatorships to benefit U.S. companies. There were, interestingly, no American jobs at stake when the United States government recently brought a trade action against the European Union on behalf of Chiquita, a descendant of the United Fruit Company—only the profits of a politically influential U.S. company.

More than four decades ago, the stakes were considerably higher.

In 1954, in response to Guatemala's newly formed democratic government's land reform proposal, U.S. troops were sent to that Central American country to protect the interests of the United Fruit Company. Noam Chomsky, speaking in Cleveland forty-five years later, noted that the U.S. government saw Guatemala's yearning for democracy and equality as "a virus that could spread."

Jacobo Arbenz, a middle-class military officer, was the second democratically elected president in Guatemalan history. His predecessor, Juan José Arevalo, had been elected after the 1944 October Revolution and had overseen the first democratic reforms in a formerly authoritarian government, but he had done little to improve the social and economic circumstances of Guatemalan peasants and workers or to challenge U.S. economic interests in the country. In the early 1950s, Arbenz took office and pushed through the legislature a bold land reform program that redistributed unused land from large landowners to Indian peasants. Although many of Arbenz's advisers were communists (none were connected to the Soviet Union, however), his land reform was fundamentally capitalistic. Land was redistributed into small plots for individual families, not into state-owned collectives. Landowners were compensated in government bonds.

However, large landowners protested not only because their unused land had been taken, but because they had lost much of their easily exploited cheap labor force, who were now working their own land. By the time the CIA overthrew Arbenz, 500,000 peasants out of a total population of three million had received land, and the numbers were still increasing. The CIA, fresh from the successful ouster of Iran's Mohammed Mossadegh, another democratically elected leader overthrown by Eisenhower, coordinated an armed rebellion in 1954 of Guatemalan "exiles" led by the right-winger Carlos Castillo Armas, marking the first CIA-backed coup in Latin America. Although Arbenz had broad popular support in Guatemala at the time of the invasion, and the antigovernment rebels had only a few hundred troops when they invaded Guatemala from Honduras, the army eventually betrayed the government because its top officers, who had enjoyed a working if somewhat strained relationship with Arbenz, feared the United States. When he discovered that he had lost the support of the army, Arbenz stepped down. Before resigning, Arbenz tried to arrange for Colonel Carlos Enrique Diaz to succeed him. He felt that Colonel Diaz, who was more conservative than himself but not reactionary, would preserve the elements of procedural democracy, if not the social democratic policies like land reform, of the last ten years. The United States refused. They (and United Fruit) wanted the "stability" that only a right-wing dictator like Castillo Armas could provide. That "stability" has caused Guatemala to be embroiled in a civil war for most of the years since. At least 200,000 Guatemalans have died.

America's foreign policy indifference to, or support of, dictators continues to this day. After a brutal junta overthrew Burma's fledgling democracy and imposed one of the world's most repressive regimes, the United States' response was tepid. Although the United States imposed sanctions, many in our country believed they did not go far enough.

In 1996 the Massachusetts state legislature passed a law that prohibited state agencies from doing business with companies that have business interests in Burma (renamed Myanmar), now a nation with one of the world's worst records of human rights abuses. Thus a huge battle was joined in Massachusetts. It became, in the words of *Washington Post* editorial page staff writer Fred Hiatt, "a battleground in one of the great conflicts of the age: local sovereignty vs. an international rule of law." Similar actions had been taken before by local and state officials in the United States, against apartheid in South Africa, for example. Several states and communities in the United States pulled pension fund investments out of South Africa and passed resolutions condemning business investment in that country. There was no international fallout, other than tremendous pressure on the white South African government. Few in the Massachusetts legislature thought that its actions toward Burma would trigger an international trade incident.

But they did. The European Union prepared an action at the World Trade Organization against the Commonwealth of Massachusetts, arguing that the state violated the rules of free trade which the United States had so forcefully argued during GATT's adoption. To change the rules of trade between and among nations because of human rights violations and repressive government should simply not be within the purview of local governments, it argued. The National Foreign Trade Council (NFTC), an organization of U.S. exporters that had joined the EU, convinced a federal judge to invalidate the Massachusetts law. Halliburton, then headed by future vice president Dick Cheney, filed a "friend of the court" (amicus) brief opposing sanctions while it had a contract for an offshore petrochemical facility. Massachusetts lost its appeal before the United States Supreme Court, which prevented the dispute from being played out at the World Trade Organization.

It is so important to implement enforceable worker and environmental standards at the core of the World Trade Organization. To date, the U.S. has free-trade agreements with six countries: Canada, Israel, Mexico, Jordan, Singapore, and Chile. Only two of these (Canada and Israel) have similar democracies with environmental and worker protections. The other four nations have much weaker commitments to democracy and have minimal worker and environmental protections. Mexico operated under one-party rule for almost all of the twentieth century, and its democracy was clouded by rampant corruption. Its labor and environmental laws are weaker than those in the United States, and even these standards are barely enforced. Jordan is a monarchy with minimal political freedoms, weak labor laws, and significantly weaker environmental protections. The Jordan Free Trade Agreement's (FTA) labor and environmental provisions are stronger on paper than any other agreement, but the enforcement of these provisions is substantially weaker than the provisions to enforce commercial rights under the agreement. Moreover, George W. Bush's administration has promised it will not act on even the weaker environmental and labor provisions. Singapore prohibits independent labor unions and it curtails many of the freedoms U.S. citizens enjoy. Chile's Pinochet-era labor law forbids unions many basic organizing rights; attempts at reform have been stymied by Pinochet supporters in the Chilean Senate since he left power more than a decade ago. Both the Singapore and Chile Free Trade Agreements were negotiated after the Jordan FTA, but neither contains the labor and environmental provisions found in the Jordan agreement.

United States willingness to enter into free-trade deals with countries that demonstrably lack political freedom should be a clarion call to human rights advocates worldwide. By "constructively engaging" with totalitarian and authoritarian governments, the United States is offering the elites of these countries financial incentives to continue repressive regimes, to limit freedom, and to crack down on workers and independent labor unions. China's entry into the WTO provides a case study in the perils of "delinking" WTO membership from a country's behavior toward its population.

China's fundamental lack of political, religious, and economic freedom calls into question China's membership in the global economic community. China is a nation of 1.2 billion people ruled by an authoritarian government with a demonstrated aversion to environmental and labor standards, and to human rights. Permitting the country to accede to the WTO was a grave mistake because WTO rules protecting worker rights, the environment, and food safety are as yet unwritten. China's participation in the WTO amid the negotiations for these protections will only pull down the standards that we hope we can convince the WTO to adopt. The Clinton administration had, somewhat disingenuously, touted the creation of its working group on labor and the environment as a major breakthrough for the World Trade Organization. In the next decade the group will finalize a set of recommendations on how best to incorporate clean air, food safety standards, and labor rights. Given the pace of reform inherent in large bureaucracies, the fight to incorporate real standards will be a difficult one; little progress had been made by these working groups between the failed Seattle and Cancún ministerials. The Bush administration, at the behest of its strongest corporate backers and most generous political contributors, has expressed its unrelenting opposition.

Those of us in Congress who want to extend to the rest of the world the same protections that we enjoy in the United States recognize (especially with an unsupportive president) how steep the hill is that we need to climb. That fight will be much more difficult when the dictatorship that rules the People's Republic of China threatens to dump hundreds of billions of dollars of goods into our market if the WTO even attempts to negotiate tough labor and environmental provisions. With China inside the WTO, the United States has lost most of the little leverage it exercised with that nation. The annual congressional vote on Most Favored Nation (MFN) status for China served as a small check on Chinese human rights violations. Accession to the WTO for the People's Republic of China took that away.

Compounding matters, the Chinese Communist Party, which has fashioned itself as a "workers' paradise," issued a statement after the conclusion of the WTO talks: "China holds that those issues that are not related to the functions of WTO, such as labour standards, should not be incorporated into the agenda." Despite WTO membership, China continues not only to repress political, religious, and labor freedoms, but also fails to open its markets as promised. China has repeatedly violated its promises on intellectual property and other commercial agreements. U.S. agriculture has been thwarted from selling crops to China by complex, changing import regulations. WTO accession for China destroys by a thousand cuts the chance for rule of law in that organization.

In East Asia, autocratic governments have coexisted, profitably for its political leaders and its wealthiest citizens, alongside free markets and generally wide-open capitalism. In China, although Communist Party leader Jiang Zemin ordered the People's Liberation Army to get rid of its businesses, almost one-third of the military's budget comes from profits from hotels, factories, pharmaceutical manufacturing, and auto plants. And the West loves doing business there. China, with its "Stalinist brand of capitalism," gives no indication that more jobs and greater wealth will loosen the grip of its Communist leaders.

Singapore, Indonesia, and Chile, for example, have all proven that you can have free markets without free people. And the largest country in the world is probably the best example. In two decades of Reagan-Bush-Clinton-Bush "constructive engagement," our trade with China is no fairer and the Chinese people are no freer. In its annual "Country Report on Human Rights Practices" issued on February 26, 1999, the United States Department of State used virtually identical language to describe the 1998 human rights record of the People's Republic of China and the Republic of Serbia, a nation with which we were at war only a few weeks later: "extrajudicial killings, . . . arbitrary arrests and detentions"; "torture." Both countries, according to our government's report, severely "restricted freedom of speech and of the press," and infringed on "freedom of worship and freedom of movement." In both countries, conditions had deteriorated from the year before. But, as California Democratic representative Nancy Pelosi said at a July 1999 news conference, "We raise a gun in Serbia, but are unwilling to raise a tariff in China."

Since June 4, 1989, when hundreds—perhaps thousands—of Chinese civilians were murdered by the People's Liberation Army on Tiananmen Square in Beijing, the U.S. government and America's largest corporations have seen China as an opportunity, an untapped economic resource. Engagement with China accommodates American business's frantic pursuit of new markets, bringing wealth to China and huge profits to Western investors.

Consumerism has saved Stalinism in China. But only the business community—not human rights groups, not international labor unions, not nongovernment organizations (NGOs)—has been allowed to engage with China. This immense increase in wealth has made the Chinese government and the People's Liberation Army more powerful and more oppressive. Some people now have more wealth, but few have more freedom. And the United States, especially our most prominent companies, has played a significant role in making that happen.

The power of corporations to weaken labor, health, and human rights standards is felt most acutely in our trade relations with the PRC. For ten years, beginning in 1989, the president notified the House of Representatives and Senate that he was renewing Most Favored Nation status for China, granting the PRC the same trading privileges that we as a nation extend to most other countries in the world. Under this procedure, Congress had sixty days from its July 2 expiration date to enact legislation revoking MFN. If Congress failed to act, China's MFN status was automatically renewed for another year. (Supporters of China on the House Ways and Means Committee in the late 1990s changed the term to Normal Trade Relations in an effort to win the public relations war.)

The annual outcome was never in doubt, because an already-threatened presidential veto meant that MFN opponents needed two-thirds of the vote in both houses of Congress (a veto-proof majority), an almost impossible scenario. Just to make sure, CEOs and their governmental affairs representatives every year swarmed over Capitol Hill, going from office to office, arguing that "constructive engagement" with Communist China was slowly edging that country away from human rights abuses, away from its roguish and belligerent behavior in the community of nations, and away from its persecution of Christians, Muslims, and Buddhists. Besides, preached these CEOs, who rarely stop anywhere on Capitol Hill except in the congressional leadership suites, MFN is good for business. As they visited the lowliest freshmen in the minority party (America's business titans must continually remind themselves that every House member has one vote) in the most remote and cramped offices in the Longworth and Cannon office buildings, they almost giddily talked of one billion Chinese, all potential customers for their companies' products. Few mentioned—publicly—the more certain and profitable prospect of China's one billion potential workers, laboring for pennies an hour, or more cheaply in forced labor camps, without the costs of fair labor standards to protect them, and as obsequious and obedient as cogs in a 3,000-year-old totalitarian machine must surely be.

In the late spring of 2000, President Clinton asked Congress to grant Permanent Normal Trade Relations (PNTR) with China. No issue has attracted a salivating corporate America to the halls of Congress the way that the proposed PNTR did: more corporate planes at National Airport; more big-name CEOs walking congressional corridors; more "astroturf lobbying" from home.* And no trade issue interests large American businesses the way that trade with China does. As Willie Sutton said about banks, "That's where the money is."

Opponents of PNTR built their case assiduously and passionately. Led by House Democratic Whip David Bonior, Nancy Pelosi (the future Democratic House leader), and Frank Wolf, a moderate-to-conservative Republican from Virginia, we argued that MFN has changed Communist China's behavior nary a whit. As Western investment has poured in, it has strengthened the Communist Party and the Chinese People's Liberation Army—making them wealthier and more powerful, and more resolved to continue their autocratic rule. Chinese dissident Wei Jingsheng, China's most prominent democracy activist, notes that much of Chinese exports come from state-owned enterprises, many of them run by the People's Liberation Army.

For a short time, the U.S. government conditioned MFN status on China improving its horrid human rights record. But in 1994, under unrelenting pressure from the U.S. Chamber of Commerce and other large business interests, President Clinton relaxed the pressure on China when he "delinked" the extension of Most Favored Nation status from the improvement of that country's abysmal human rights record. From the imprisonment in November 1995 of Wei Jingsheng, to the separate one-day trials, convictions, and ten-plus-year sentences in December 1998 for dissidents Wang Youcai, Xu Wenli, Zhang Shanguang, and Qin Yongmin, to the attacks on reli-

---

* "Astroturf lobbying" was a phrase coined in the early 1990s when political consultants, looking for work between elections, suggested to tobacco conglomerates, health insurance companies, and other special-interest groups that they could employ an avalanche of letters and a flurry of activities to create the illusion that there was grassroots support for the corporate position.

gious organizations at Christmas 2000, the gerontocrats in China's Communist Party leadership have declared war on democracy. Zhang, for example, was sentenced to ten years in prison by a court in the southern province of Hunan after a two-hour-and-ten-minute trial for "illegally providing intelligence to foreign organizations" (he had spoken by telephone to a reporter from the U.S.-funded Radio Free Asia about farmers' protests). In November and December 1998, six months after President Clinton's "successful" trip to China, which included a debate between the president and Chinese Communist Party leader Jiang Zemin over the progress of democratic reforms, the Communist Chinese government arrested at least thirty political democracy activists and detained scores of church leaders. It issued strong new directives warning singers, computer software developers, and film directors that if their behavior "endangers national security," it could land them in prison. And America's corporate leaders continue to do China's bidding in Washington, and convince our government to give that country favorable trading privileges.

Throughout the PNTR debate and through the cooling and thawing of U.S.-China relations, the Chinese government's offensive against Tibet has continued unabated. Amnesty International, the respected human rights group, has reported on the central government's assault on Tibetan culture and the Buddhist religion, and has released the names of hundreds of Tibetans, many of whom have spoken out for Tibetan independence, who are in Chinese prisons. Some are as young as twelve, others as old as eighty. The ethnic cleansing in Tibet is not much different from Slobodan Milosevich's actions in Kosovo, but our business leaders and our newspaper publishers have remained silent.

Our trade balance with China continues to worsen as China erects almost impenetrable barriers to many U.S. products. The U.S. trade deficit with China climbed from only $100 million in 1985 to more than $10 billion in 1990, to $34 billion in 1995, to $60 billion in 1998, and to over $75 billion when Congress passed PNTR in 2000—almost 800 times the level of thirteen years earlier. It passed the $100 billion mark—by far the biggest bilateral trade deficit any two countries have ever had—in 2003. And since President Clinton in 1994 officially "delinked" trade policy and human rights in our dealings with China, human rights violations have increased markedly. Unquestionably, our trade policies cost Americans jobs—large numbers of generally good-paying jobs. Economists in the first Bush administration calculated that one billion dollars in trade represented 13,000 jobs, most of them high-caliber export jobs: a one billion dollar trade surplus created 13,000 jobs; conversely, a one billion dollar trade deficit lost 13,000 jobs for a nation. The trade deficits contributed significantly to the United States' net loss, during George W. Bush's first three years in office, of three million jobs, by far the worst job performance for an American president since Herbert Hoover. In my state of Ohio, one in six manufacturing jobs has been lost since January 20, 2001. Most important and most tragically, the overwhelming majority of these jobs are unlikely to return. Unlike past recessions and stagnant economic times, most jobs lost—especially in manufacturing—were temporary; with economic recovery, most of the jobs returned. According to Erica Groshen and Simon Potter, writing for a Federal Reserve Bank publication *Current Issues in Economics and Finance,* 2002–2004 is very different. Fully 79 percent of these jobs losses are "structural," meaning they are permanently lost, and a huge number of them have gone overseas.

More than one-third of China's exports go to the United States. Visit any clothing, sporting goods, telecommunications, electronics, or toy store in the United States and see the evidence. In contrast, only 2 percent of our exports go to China. We actually sell more, as a nation, to Singapore, a nation with about one three-hundredth the pop-ulation of China. In my seven terms in Congress, our aggregate trade deficit with China has reached almost $1 trillion. And that deficit fig-ure does not even include the increasing exports, especially textiles, that China is transshipping through other countries, many of them in Africa, to avoid U.S. quotas and evade bilateral trade accounting.

There is more. In late 2003 I spoke with Mike Siegal, a steel service executive from Cleveland. He outlined to me the increased economic power that China holds in the world's economy—reaching well be-yond the burgeoning trade deficit numbers. The Chinese are buying up large amounts of natural resources in the United States—natural gas, coal, other minerals, even U.S. energy companies. "China has to put its U.S. dollars somewhere," he shrugged. He pointed out that the increased price that his suppliers and customers pay for raw materials—especially for coal and natural gas—and scrap steel far ex-ceed the costs of steel tariffs and increased health-care costs, even when you factor in prescription drugs. Then, he added, it only gets worse. While China's flood of Western currency drives prices of natu-ral resources upward in the United States, these increased costs to China manufacturers have had little impact on prices of Chinese products but a major impact on prices of goods produced by U.S. manufacturers in the United States—again deepening the U.S.-China trade imbalance.

Dan Imbrogno, the president of Ohio Screw Products in Elyria, Ohio, showed me a small metal part that his company has been man-ufacturing for years. With annual sales of about $8 million, the loss of a $500,000 order to China was a big blow to this company of seventy-five to eighty employees. "I was a tried-and-true free trader," he told Harold Meyerson of the *Washington Post*. "But you put details into the theory and it falls apart. When the Chinese government manipulates its currency and subsidizes its manufacturers, the theory doesn't work. It's how we built our country. It's how European and East Asian countries built theirs."

Free traders and defenders of the status quo point out that things are changing, that China has now become the world's third largest importer (only the United States and Germany import more). They neglect to say, however, that much of the Chinese imports are, as under NAFTA, energy, components, and machine tools that will be used for manufacturing plants. They simply are not importing consumer goods that would raise the standard of living of their people. And, more important, fully 85 percent of U.S.-China trade is represented by Chinese exports to the United States, while only 15 percent is United States exports to China.

Nothing much seems to change with the Chinese: imprisonment of political prisoners and repression of dissent; persecution of Tibetans; forced abortion and sterilization; execution of prisoners to feed a growing organ-harvesting business; violation of accepted international norms in conduct of foreign policy; and an extraordinarily one-sided bilateral trade relationship. But because there are major profits in China, America's corporate leaders continue to do China's bidding in Washington.

By the time of the May 2000 House vote on Permanent Normal Trade Relations, the stakes were very, very high. Bilateral trade between the United States and China had exceeded $100 billion annually, although five-sixths of it went in one direction, to the detriment of American workers. At the same time, U.S. business investment in China went from just $350 million in 1990 to $25 billion in 1996 to more than $30 billion in 2000, an almost hundredfold increase in less than a decade.

America's China lobby was ready. Plenty of people—most of them trained by taxpayers in positions of prominence in the highest echelons of the American government—have made plenty of money advancing the cause of China in Washington, D.C.: former secretary of state Henry Kissinger, former secretary of state Alexander Haig, former secretary of state Cyrus Vance, former secretary of state Lawrence Eagleburger. They have all worked for, or consulted with, American companies who want to invest in China. Most export back to the United States; many provide their technology, some of it defense-related, much of it high-tech, to the Chinese in exchange for access to China's very cheap, highly disciplined, and coercively obedient labor force.

Lots of other prominent Americans have pitched in to help the Chinese government: former secretary of state George Shultz, former secretary of state Warren Christopher, former United States trade representative Carla Hills, former United States trade representative William Brock, former United States trade representative Robert Strauss, former Senate majority leader Howard Baker, former National Security Council advisor Brent Scowcroft, former secretary of defense and now vice president Richard Cheney, former ambassador to the United Nations Bill Richardson, former ambassador to China and United Auto Workers president Leonard Woodcock. The overwhelming majority of them are Republicans (the Communists in China especially seem to like to do business with America's big-business party), but a few are very prominent Democrats too—Vance, Woodcock, Strauss. Many of America's best-known government officials have fostered a whole new twist on the age-old adage from Foggy Bottom, "Politics stops at the water's edge."

It is evident that America's lobbyists for China have much in common. They are mostly prominent government officials with foreign policy credentials that policymakers and the public respect. Always willing to talk to the media about China, they write columns for America's most respected newspapers and journals. When they talk to the American media, the United States Congress, and the American public, they can certainly speak for the People's Republic of China much more credibly than Chinese leaders can speak for themselves.

Corporate America hires these former officials for their clout—with Congress, with the media, and, interestingly, with the Chinese themselves. Clout with Congress is not difficult because most members of Congress, in both Houses, lack a depth of knowledge of foreign policy and will listen all too eagerly to prominent former officials. Clout with the media, which lap up well-delivered quotes from people who learned how to deliver them when they worked for the United States government, is also not difficult, especially when many in the media either do not realize or neglect to factor in these former officials' clients. And their clout with China is well earned. That clout, as pointed out by journalist John Judis, is based in part on their history of statements about China to the American media. You had to be friendly to China when you were in office, Judis said. And you have to be friendly now as a consultant, and that means defending Chinese rulers regardless of their actions. Former ambassador to China James Lilley said, "If you want to deal in China, you will sing their tune. This can take a number of forms. It can take the form of bringing congressional visitors over [to China]. It can take the form of an op-ed piece in the *New York Times*. It can take the form of a speech. It can take the form of lobbying Congress."

Henry Kissinger is Communist China's best foil. A frequent guest op-ed writer for the *Washington Post* when we were debating annual MFN and permanent NTR status, Kissinger was typically identified at the bottom of the columns as "former U.S. secretary of state," as if the reader did not already know that. There was nary a mention of his consulting firm or his clients; he was writing only as an expert and a statesman. It was only after repeated calls to the *Post* from many of us on Capitol Hill that Kissinger's byline was tagged with the name of his consulting firm. Today, in Kissinger's regular op-ed missives to the *Post*, he is identified only as "president of Kissinger Associates, an international consulting firm"; even when he writes about China and our trade policy, there is never a mention of his clients and his business interests in that country. Kissinger is credited, at least in part, with the 1994 Clinton administration decision that delinked human rights from Most Favored Nation status for China, a major victory for American business and for the Chinese government.

The more good things you say about China, according to former ambassador Lilley, the more doors you can open in Beijing for your client. The better lobbying you do *for* China, the more success you will enjoy for your client *with* China. This perverse situation provides every financial incentive for Kissinger, Scowcroft, Hills, et al. to always speak well of Communist China, no matter what its government's offenses. Besides, the Chinese tell them, American business would have such an easier time of it in China if America would simply quit putting pressure on the Chinese government, and if Americans would stop their unfair criticism of it. Our former(ly) respected government officials dutifully pass that information on—to a business-dominated Congress, to a gullible and big-eared media, and to a much more skeptical public.

These former top American elected and appointed government officials are there, as the Scowcroft Group advertises, to develop "market entry strategies" for companies seeking opportunities around the world, especially in the world's largest nation. Most justify their fence jumping, much as did Bob Dole with the Chilean salmon farmers (see chapter 1), by equating the interests of large American companies with the interests of American workers and investors at home—a sort of "What's good for GM is good for America" philosophy.

In late September 1999, *Fortune* magazine held "the most important international event in our magazine's sixty-nine-year history" in

Shanghai. The *Fortune* Global Forum's "China: The Next Fifty Years" was an invitation-only celebration, attended by the CEOs of the largest corporations in the United States, that focused "on the practical realities of doing business in China today and into the next century." Speakers included Jiang Zemin, former American secretary of state Henry Kissinger, and former U.S. trade representative Mickey Kantor. After the three-day gala, several of the CEOs journeyed to Beijing for anniversary commemorations of fifty years of Communism; they watched the Chinese military parade at Tiananmen Square, the site of the student massacre by the Chinese government precisely ten years earlier. Presumably the question of "Who lost China fifty years earlier?" was not addressed.

The chief executive officer of Time-Warner, attending the ceremonies at Tiananmen Square, presented a bust of Abraham Lincoln to Jiang Zemin because the Chinese Communist official likes to quote the former American president.* China's leaders reciprocated and expressed their appreciation to 170 world leaders by, according to the official Xinhua news agency, presenting them, at the end of the year 2000, "New Millennium" gifts of paving stones from Tiananmen Square, presumably without reference to the murders of the earlier democracy protestors. Queen Elizabeth and President Clinton were two of the recipients. Several days later, Jiang further showed gratitude to Time-Warner by closing the distribution network for *Time* magazine in China.

Almost every major American corporation belongs to the U.S.-

---

* Some Lincoln quotations that were probably not engraved on the bust: "As I would not be a slave, so I would not be a master"; "Those who deny freedom to others deserve it not for themselves"; "Why should there not be a patient confidence in the ultimate justice of the people?"; "Public opinion in this country is everything"; "He can compress the most words into the smallest idea of any man I ever met."

China Business Council, whose members—America's most prominent chief executive officers and presidents of our nation's largest companies—in essence lobby for the Communist Chinese in the halls of Congress. The government of the People's Republic of China does not lobby Congress for MFN or other desirable goodies from America; they don't have to, because some of our country's wealthiest people are doing it for them. And they know how to do it well.

During the MFN and PNTR debates, the U.S.-China Business council said that congressional defeat of China trade advantages would be a "declaration of economic war." One CEO presciently explained to me that thousands of our constituents would blame Congress for the economic turmoil that would surely occur in the United States. He patiently warned me that our less-than-responsible head-in-the-sand action would cause massive layoffs of American workers.

But the facts simply did not add up. Loss of American jobs? Our trade deficit with China continues to climb, approaching $200 billion annually, with no end in sight. We simply are not in the game when it comes to exports to China. We sell more to Taiwan—with less than one-fiftieth (!) the population of China—than we do to its huge neighbor. Japan and South Korea each import more American-made products than does China. And, according to John Maggs of the *Journal of Commerce,* U.S. exports to Brazil, Poland, and a dozen other countries are increasing more rapidly than our exports to China. China's economy is growing very fast, but its U.S. imports are not anywhere near approaching that level of growth; the Chinese government will not let that happen. We are simply not part of China's economic success story, except as a buyer of whatever they want to sell us, and there is no reason to believe we ever will be.

In 1997 Boeing made a very lucrative deal with the Chinese, selling them a big order of airplanes and giving the Chinese in return some joint production in China—where Boeing could manufacture at very low cost compared to what it pays its union machinists in Seattle—and a significant part of its heretofore top-secret aerospace technology. In addition to being a large American company transferring potential national security technology to a potential enemy, Boeing is in fact also hurting its own long-term prospects as a company. China will surely, at some point, use their newly acquired airplane technology to launch its own aircraft industry, by which time they will have no need for Boeing's services. Perhaps they will even compete with Boeing in the world aircraft market. But that will probably be ten or fifteen years away, and of little consequence to Boeing's present-day top management, who by then will have landed softly and comfortably with their golden parachutes.

Thus, while Americans are deservedly proud of our high-tech successes, China is rapidly catching up, with the unwitting—and sometimes witting—assistance of U.S. companies and the U.S. government. U.S. export earnings from technology have declined over the last five years, while Chinese export earnings from technology from the United States have increased dramatically—up 34 percent in 1998, and another 57 percent in 1999. In other words, we are—even in the field of technology, an area where America consistently has claimed superiority and an expertise on which we base much of our future—buying much more from China than we are selling. China announced in late 2000 that its worldwide exports of computers for the first half of that year had increased 666 percent, reaching almost one million, while their imports fell 9 percent, to only 27,000. As economist Charles W. McMillion and South Carolina Democratic senator Ernest "Fritz" Hollings pointed out, while high-tech U.S. companies continue to invest in China and sell their products back into the United States (again demonstrating that it is the one billion Chinese workers that interest them, not the one billion Chinese consumers), the Chinese are demanding more and more technology from them.

The Chinese Communist government has already put this technology to good use. State-run China Mobile—soon to become the world's largest mobile phone company—is expanding outside China. It has sold $100 million in mobile phones to the United States, while the United States exports no mobile phones to China. Yet American and other Western high-tech companies continue to be, in Senator Hollings's words, "exceedingly arrogant and shortsighted in acceding to these demands from their Chinese 'partners' and officials."

Before its merger with Daimier, Chrysler was offered a similar kind of deal. China's invitation for Chrysler to invest in China came with a few strings: give us your design technology and tell us about your manufacturing processes. Chrysler CEO Robert Eaton, a big China trade backer who walked the corridors of Congress on behalf of MFN and PNTR, said no thanks to Beijing. "They want us to set them up as a world-class competitor to Chrysler, and pay for it too."

At least Eaton was smart enough, or cared enough, to know what Communist China was doing to his company and his country. Some other American companies apparently did not act so honorably. "Western businesspeople," Laogai Foundation founder Harry Wu told a group of us in my office, "start salivating when they contemplate the profits they hope to harness in China."

Americans doing business in China are not the only ones who see green. Prior to the annexation of Hong Kong by China in July 1997, most of Hong Kong's business elite had already made book with the Communist Chinese, although one could certainly make the case that their proximity to the People's Liberation Army and the Chinese police made their case a bit more urgent than that of America's big-business class. Their deal, some thought, was: you let us enjoy the freedoms we have had under self-rule, and we will continue to make lots of money for Hong Kong and now for China. But the deal from China, as July 1 approached, became something very different: you make a lot of money for us, and we will let you do your business freely. Period. Don't expect political freedom to come with it.

Hong Kong businessmen and businesswomen, and it might be fair to say many corporate leaders throughout the world, seem to prefer a Singapore-style business environment, suggests Stan Sesser, a senior fellow of the Human Rights Center at Berkeley: few civil liberties for the people, but ample room and freedom for business to make money. Labor unions are repressed, protests are banned, freedoms are restricted. But, says Sesser, the government of Singapore has "created a dual system of information, unlimited for corporations, but restricted for ordinary Singaporeans, who can't own satellite dishes and must channel their Internet correspondence through a government computer that weeds out unwelcome web sites." The new chief executive of the Hong Kong Special Administrative Region, Tung Chee-hwa, trumpeted the success of Singapore and held it up as a model for others. Upon his selection, which involved banning the democratically elected Legislative Council and allowing only 400 Beijing-appointed representatives to vote, the Hong Kong–based *Far Eastern Economic Review,* the sister paper of the *Wall Street Journal,* purred, "The entire exercise of producing the first chief executive has been heartening."

As U.S. business leaders continue to make their case for expanded trade with China, the U.S.-China Business Council raises the age-old and largely inaccurate specter of the Smoot-Hawley Act of 1930 (see chapter 7). Revocation of annual MFN—or later defeat of PNTR—could lead to retaliation, a worldwide trade war, political instability, and economic depression, they somberly warn. Echoing those concerns but ignoring the trade balance and one-way nature of Sino-American trade, President Clinton wrote to me in response to a letter I sent to him in the summer of 1997: "Revoking MFN would . . . close one of the world's emerging markets to our exports and endanger an estimated 170,000 American jobs." Earlier, President Clinton, in a

June 1996 letter to members of Congress, said failure to extend Most Favored Nation status to China would "sever our economic relationship and seriously undermine our capacity to engage China on matters of vital concern such as non-proliferation, human rights, trade, and Taiwan relations." This president, and his predecessors and successor in the White House, neglected to mention China's unwillingness to enforce U.S. trade law toward slave labor.

The final paragraph of the Smoot-Hawley Act forbids the importing of any goods produced by forced labor:

> "Forced labor," as herein used, shall mean all work or service which is exacted from any person under the menace of any penalty for its nonperformance, and for which the worker does not offer himself voluntarily.

Thanks to the efforts of Chinese dissident Harry Wu, who had studied the Chinese *laogai** system for years, the U.S. Customs Service in 1991 impounded wrenches and steel pipes that were parts produced by forced labor for Chinese diesel engines. The engines were never released for sale in the United States.

---

* *Laogai* is the Mandarin term for forced labor system; the Laogai Foundation was founded in the United States by Wu, who is almost certainly the world's leading expert on the *laogai*. He estimates that more than 50 million people have been sent to these camps since 1949. The camps were modeled after Soviet leader Joseph Stalin's gulag when the Soviets and Chinese were on better terms. The camps, the punishment, and the death still go on, in Wu's words, "subsidized by corporations, subsidized by the World Bank, subsidized by all the governments that encourage trade with China." For their first thirty years, the *laogai*, the largest system of concentration camps in human history, served as a primitive trash heap for alleged political and civil criminals. But now, Wu says, "these camps are part of the Chinese gross domestic product." Stalinism, in its uniquely Chinese way, lives on, yet American business and political leaders persistently turn a blind eye to these outrages.

Wu had been a prisoner in the *laogai* system from 1960–1979, and, after emigrating to the United States in the mid-1980s, he set up the Laogai Foundation. He returned to China surreptitiously three times, inspecting many of the camps, taking photographs, talking to prisoners. The third time he was caught, detained for two months, and returned to the United States amid international cries for his release.

The camp where the aforementioned engines were made is located in Yunnan Province in south-central China. Wu found that the region had at least 1,000 prisoners in forced labor. His alerting the public, Congress, and the administration kept out of the United States the engines that were made in that camp, but unfortunately, nothing much changed after the diesel engine incident. Neither the Bush nor Clinton nor second Bush administrations seemed much interested after that incident in enforcing the anti–slave labor sections of U.S. law.

In December 1998 Chinese president Jiang Zemin inadvertently helped MFN opponents build our case. Speaking to Communist Party members at the Great Hall of the People in Beijing the day after the commencement of the political trials of three well-known Chinese dissidents, Jiang pronounced that reforms would not mean steps toward democracy; they would mean only more economic growth and prosperity from the top down. No relaxing of the clutch of the Communist Party. No weakening of the grip of the People's Liberation Army. No loosening of the bonds of totalitarianism. In short, no Western-style democracy. "Our political system must not be shaken," he thundered. Decidedly wearing his other hat as general secretary of the Communist Party, Jiang reassured his party faithful, "The Western mode of political systems must never be copied."

The cardinal principles of China's brand of Communism, the autocrat promised, would remain inviolate: dominance by the Communist Party, allegiance to Mao Zedong's thought, adherence to Marxist-Leninism, faithfulness to the socialist path. Western democratic values had no place in China. The speaker of the National People's Party Congress, Li Peng, affirmed, "If an organization's purpose is to promote a multi-party system in China and negate the leadership prerogatives of the Chinese Communist Party, then it will not be permitted to exist."

Neither Jiang Zemin nor Li Peng, when speaking to fellow Communists, suggested slowing private development or restricting Western investment. Unlike U.S. business leaders who pronounce American investment in China as the catalyst for bringing democracy to China, Jiang obviously sees no link between the two. Bring on the investors, he urges, but keep out the democrats. Help us create wealth, especially for the Communist Party and the People's Liberation Army, but don't try to tell us that human rights and freedom of speech will work in China. Let business make decisions that will add to their profits, but don't allow workers a fair wage, a safe workplace, or any semblance of self-government.

In December 1998, Jiang Zemin told the *New York Times*, "We must be vigilant against infiltration, subversive activities, and separatist activities of international and domestic hostile forces." Jiang said that China must "fight against factors disrupting social stability and nip them in the bud." Simply put, the nation that has earned the label of "Stalinist capitalist" wants to continue that way, and no number of Western business ventures there will change its course. Six months later, in June 1999, Jiang reiterated his hard-line position. In a speech marking a Communist Party holiday, he told fellow party delegates that communism would win out over capitalism, and that "China was doomed if party members ever lost faith in communism." Stay the course, he firmly reassured his faithful.

In a 2002 meeting at the central government's Zhong Nan Hai

complex in Beijing, Chinese premier Zhu Rongji told me and a few other members of Congress about "the unbalanced psychology" of protestors: "The so-called democratic elements have made contacts with workers who want to form trade unions. . . . Everyday on my desk I have a bulletin telling me where workers have taken to the streets in protest." The premier told us that Chinese entry into the World Trade Organization would make it even more difficult to impose any environmental standards or labor standards on the world's economies. "It would have been impossible for China to have registered such a level of success if we had adopted your suggestions on labor and the environment," he asserted.

Jiang Zemin. Li Peng. Zhu Rongji. The three most powerful men in the government of this country of 1.3 billion people have told the world: Prosperity in China is not going to lead to political freedom. It's not the plan. We don't do it that way.

None of this should come as a surprise, considering the evidence. Harry Wu said, "Capitalism must never be equated with democracy. This is a very American belief—making money produces freedom and justice and equality. Don't believe it about China. My homeland is mired in thousands of years of rule by one bully at a time, whether you call him emperor or chairman. Don't be fooled by electronics or air-conditioning." Conservative trade expert and free trader Edward Luttwak, a senior fellow at the Center for Strategic and International Studies, cautioned against believing that economic activity in China equates to political freedom. "Free markets and less-free societies go hand in hand," he asserted.

On the surface, logic might suggest that more jobs in an economy and greater wealth in a society would mean more openness, a growing middle class, a stronger desire for self-rule, and an eventual acquiescence by the powerful to share their wealth and their power. But oppressive governments have no reason to share the wealth and create a middle class and absolutely every reason not to open their society and empower their workers. As China continued to trade more with the United States and watch its trade surplus grow, human rights violations continued to mount: the report found killings, torture of prisoners, and forced confessions; there were new regulations covering the Internet and the publishing industry; several newspapers and social organizations were shut down. After PNTR passed Congress, repression in China continued unabated. China eagerly signed onto the war on terrorism because it dovetailed nicely with its repression of the Muslim Uigar population in western China, where the country is adopting a forced assimilation policy similar to the one it used in Tibet. Tax protests and retiree demonstrations against China's failure to meet its obligations and pay its workers and retirees have met with stiff police and military resistance. Independent labor union activists continue to be jailed and working conditions remain severe and dangerous. For example, an estimated 10,000 workers perish in China's coal mines each year; in contrast, 42 U.S. coal miners died in 2001.

So much for the CEO's arguments that MFN and more unregulated trade with China will set China down the road to democracy and a pluralist society. Philip Tose, the chairman of one of Asia's largest investment banks, extolled the virtues of "strong government—some would call it dictatorship." Strong governments, he continued, "deliver much better economic growth." Why, one might ask, would capitalists from Western democracies want change in China? Why change something that works for them? Why democracy, when authoritarianism delivers?

Lewis Lapham, the editor of *Harper's,* tells a story of his visit to the 1998 World Economic Forum in Davos, Switzerland. An earnest young man from the People's Republic of China approached him and said, "You know in China we're spending $750 billion in infrastructures but in the last two months we laid off one million railroad workers. You could say that our lack of democracy is a blessing. In Europe or America there would be arguments." Who wants that to change— the Chinese Communist government? The People's Liberation Army? American corporate investors?

Business leaders in the industrial democracies continue to petition their democratically elected governments to ignore human rights abuses and look beyond China's aberrant behavior. "Business, after all, is business," United States Trade Representative Charlene Barshefsky told me and others at a closed-door briefing of House Commerce Committee members in June 1999. While the philosophy of China's Communist Party leadership might seem anathema to American and Western capitalist business principles, it has not been difficult for them to do business with one another. It should come as no surprise that Western businesspeople much prefer the reliable and predictable constancy of China and its autocratic government over the unreliability and uncertainty of, say, India's messy and unpredictable democracy. After all, as Wei Jingsheng said, "U.S. businessmen think they can make big profits by supporting the Communists in China."

Former United States trade representative Carla Hills—who negotiated NAFTA for President George H. W. Bush—was equally blunt with me. On a panel we shared at a Council of Foreign Relations briefing, I mentioned a study released by the National Labor Committee that showed hourly wages and working conditions of Chinese workers. The report detailed—with plentiful corroborating evidence—that workers making products for Huffy, Kathie Lee/Wal-Mart, Nike, K-Mart, and others were paid as little as 13 cents an hour. In front of a conservative, Republican crowd, Hills scoffed at my assertion, scolded me for "spreading rumors and misinformation like that," and informed me that U.S. companies in China, according to the American Chamber of Commerce in Beijing, pay an average of $4 an hour. Many in the audience, made up of business lobbyists, think-tank academicians, and economics writers—almost all free traders—knowingly and affirmingly nodded their heads. They knew she had to be right; she was one of them, while I was a protectionist interloper who just did not understand the global economy.

She neglected to tell the whole story. An American Chamber of Commerce survey of wages, based on responses from forty-eight self-selected U.S.-based companies in Beijing, found the average worker paid by these companies made $7,716 U.S. dollars annually. But U.S. companies rarely own their manufacturing facilities. Nike, for example, subcontracts with at least fifty factories with more than 100,000 workers making about 30 cents an hour. They are not included in these companies' calculations of average Nike salaries, because they are not technically Nike employees. Only those actually on the Nike payroll, many of them Americans, almost all of them in higher-level jobs, are included in Hills's $4 per hour claim.

So when America's CEOs lobbied so hard for PNTR, and piously told us that their investments in China will inexorably lead to a freer, more democratic China, are we to believe that is what they really want? Do they want their $2-a-day Chinese workers to be better paid? Do they want their generally docile and obedient Chinese workers to be empowered in the workplace to speak out and demand worker safety? Do they want their Chinese workforce to be free to choose an independent trade union and sit down at a bargaining table and ne-gotiate as equals?

Of course not. Barry Rogstad, president of the American Business Conference, a trade association of high-growth companies whose top priority is expanded free trade, told us at a Congressional Economic Leadership Institute luncheon in June 1999 that it is "sheer craziness to make another country change its behavior." Referring more than once to establishing rules for global commerce as "imperialism," he dismissively called labor standards and environmental safeguards "merely social policy." Perhaps, he might aver, protecting intellectual property rights and convincing another country to change its behavior regarding those property rights are something different.

The Communist government saves its most brutal repression for workers and for activists who attempt to promote unionism, surely making China a more attractive place for Western investment. In his 1997 book *One World, Ready or Not: The Manic Logic of Global Capitalism,* William Greider wrote:

> The promise of a democratic evolution requires special skepticism if the theory is being promoted by economic players *who actually benefit from the opposite conditions* [emphasis mine]—the enterprise doing business in low-cost labor markets where the absence of democratic rights makes it much easier to suppress wages. A corporation that has made strategic investments based on the cost advantages offered by repressive societies can hardly be expected to advocate their abolition.

Western investors have chosen to send their tens of billions of dollars of capital to the People's Republic of China for a reason. Those who are best able to effect change—the Chinese Communist Party, the People's Liberation Army, and American CEOs—clearly do not want change. The Chinese Communist Party likes the system the way it is. The People's Liberation Army likes the system the way it is. American CEOs like the system the way it is.

And China, after congressional passage of PNTR, continues to prove it. In August 2000, in the irony of all ironies, Chinese customs officials seized 16,000 copies of *The Clinton Years,* a 227-page coffee-table book of black-and-white photographs of the president of the

United States. The Chinese government confiscated the books, which were printed in English for sale in the United States, from a bindery in Schenzen in south China after they had been printed in Hong Kong. The officials' objection was a picture of Clinton in 1994 shaking hands with the Dalai Lama. Interestingly, the U.S. president, out of deference to the Chinese Communists, received the Tibetan spiritual leader in the vice president's office, not the Oval Office. Human Rights Watch wryly commented that the Chinese were now "censoring what Americans read."

Six months after Congress rejected the appeals of religious activists in the United States and passed PNTR, China stepped up its persecution of religious groups. In the city of Wenzhou as many as 1,000 temples, churches, and ancestral halls were shut down or forced to register with the government. One church was leveled by explosives by local officials; another was attacked with sledgehammers. Two other Falun Gong (a religious movement) members died in police custody, bringing the number of deaths of movement members to at least seventy-four.

And, in a storm of even more revisionist history about the Tiananmen Square massacre, Foreign Ministry spokesman Zhu Bangzao said, in January 2001, "Any attempt to play up the matter again and disrupt China by the despicable means of fabricating materials and distorting facts will be futile." The crackdown, he said, "was highly necessary to the stability and development of China."

Five people—perhaps members of the Falun Gong, although its leaders denied it—set fire to themselves on the eve of the Chinese New Year. The Chinese government confiscated the film footage of their deaths from a CNN crew. A few days later, the Chinese government used the footage to discredit Falun Gong and build support for the government's actions taken against them and other dissidents, malcontents, and troublemakers.

And it did not really matter what China promised to the world, or what the world did for China. On July 13, 2001, the People's Republic of China was officially notified that the 2008 summer Olympic Games would be held in Beijing, which won the competition over Toronto, Sydney, and Paris. Western commentators soberly opined that bringing the Olympics to China would open up the country, shine more light on its oppressive activities, and encourage China to clean up its human rights abuses—from its labor camps to its repression aimed at the country's religious organizations. Yet, even in the wake of Beijing's selection, the Communist government continued its business as usual. Two Chinese-American scholars were seized as hostages. According to human rights groups, hundreds of Falun Gong members were arrested before the end of the summer, forty-five were sentenced to terms up to thirteen years, and four were given life sentences. The harvesting of the organs of executed "criminals," many of them political prisoners, went on unabated. And still, Western politicians, their corporate allies, and their pundit apologists in America's corporate-owned media predict that our concessions to China—on trade, with the WTO, and now with the Olympics—will improve human rights in the People's Republic of China. But it never seems to work out that way. We had given them PNTR. The world had given them the Olympics. Nothing changed.

In fact, increased economic activity and foreign investment in the People's Republic of China seems to have led to a new category of political and economic crimes, often punishable by imprisonment and death. A report of the International Labor Fund, *U.S.-China Relations, 1989–1999: Ten Years of Constructive Engagement?* notes:

> Certain types of rights abuses, such as restrictions on freedom of expression and association, arbitrary detention, lack of due process of law, torture and arbitrary application of the

death penalty remain chronic in China. Other rights abuses, notably the abuses of workers in light manufacturing industries in south China, are the result of increased commercial engagement. These abuses include practices that are chronic to sweatshop industries everywhere, including excessive overtime, arbitrary fines and other punishments, and exposure to hazardous chemicals and workplace conditions. However, these problems are exacerbated by China's unique system of internal migration controls, which may effectively bond the worker to the factory by giving the employer control over her residence permit.

To Wei Jingsheng, China's most respected democrat, there is only one solution, and that is economic. The United States should no longer provide to the Chinese government or the People's Liberation Army the very valuable technology that American companies are all too eager to sell and that the U.S. government has been all too willing to allow. As a nation, China's most prominent dissident told us, we should restrict Chinese imports to the United States. Even the probusiness Cleveland *Plain Dealer* acknowledged in an editorial that "U.S. trade practices may be subsidizing a better material life for the Chinese people but also prolonging political repression."

On a warm spring day in 2000 in Democratic Whip David Bonior's office, a group of us talked with Wei Jingsheng about PNTR. He had just been expelled from China after serving two years of a second decade-long prison sentence. Formerly an electrician at the Beijing Zoo, he had spent most of the previous twenty years in prison, having been released briefly in 1993 when the People's Republic of China was lobbying to be the host country of the 2000 Olympics. He was returned to prison later that same year. Now, he was in poor health, and Chinese Communist leaders did not want him to die in one of their prisons. He had recovered fairly well from a very serious illness, and had just come to us from a Canadian hospital. He was a soft-spoken but driven man, one who had not a moment to spare in his quest to change his country. His doctors wanted him to slow down, but he would have none of that.

"The only beneficiaries in my country of Most Favored Nation trading status," he told us, "are China's state-owned enterprises and the enterprises operated by the families of the bureaucrats. MFN actually inhibits and stunts the development of any free market enterprises in China, the most open and dynamic part of the Chinese economy, because all of the trade with the West goes through state-owned enterprises and the People's Liberation Army. All the profits of the state-owned enterprises simply feed the vast mechanism of state suppression, and are also used in the development of weapons and defense equipment."

He talked to us about the significance of America's trade deficit with China. Our then-$75-billion-and-growing trade deficit with China subsidized China's purchases and political and diplomatic activities in Europe. The Chinese Communists, he told us, need America's money, because the Chinese have a trade deficit with virtually every other Western, democratic, industrialized, trading partner. Wei explained that the Chinese government, recognizing the importance of driving a wedge into any possible Western solidarity and shared values, "uses this sum of money from exports to the United States to place large numbers of orders with key European countries. These large orders convince European countries to break out of the common foreign policies shared with the United States. . . . Not only in the policy of human rights but also in the fields of other official policy, the Chinese Communist government is practicing 'let's make a deal politics' among American allies with increasing efficacy and frequency."

Here is how it works. We give China Permanent Normal Trading privileges. In spite of their promises, they keep their markets closed to us. We run up huge bilateral trade deficits with China. The People's Republic of China takes the money—now more than $120 billion, and growing—and spends it in Europe, winning friends and influencing governments. We therefore have no leverage against China when they close their markets, smuggle AK-47s into San Francisco, exploit child labor, and destabilize south Asia and the Middle East with nuclear arms sales. Our European allies—where change runs counter to their economic interests—shrug when we ask them for help. If we retaliate in any way—Bill Clinton, George Bush, Henry Kissinger, and America's CEOs sternly warn us—China might isolate us by not buying our exports. Our experts somberly advise us that we must stay on this merry-go-round.

But wait. The Chinese hardly buy from us anyway. We export more to Belgium and its eleven million people every year than we do to China and its 1.2 billion people. And the Chinese would find it very, very difficult to unload in other countries $150 billion worth of goods that they now sell to the United States. This scam, or, in the words of Wei Jingsheng, "this type of dollar diplomacy has successfully destroyed the alliance of Western governments on the question of human rights."

Wei Jingsheng's toughest words during the PNTR debate were reserved for China's dealings with American business leaders. "American corporate executives serve as the vanguard of the Chinese Communist revolution in America," Wei told me as we walked through the Rayburn House Office Building one day. Rather jolting words to hear, to be sure, especially because all of us have seen the shamelessness of many of America's proudest CEOs scurrying around the corridors of Congress looking for members of Congress to convert. "Because the opportunities for American business to gain

access to the Chinese market are controlled by the Chinese government," Wei says, "many of the American businessmen are forced to
serve the political purposes of the Chinese Communists. They use
their influence and resources to conduct lobbying activities for the
Chinese government. This severely influences American foreign policy." An optimistic man by nature, Wei smiled and said that by defeating PNTR and invoking fair trade principles with Beijing, "the
initiative and power to eliminate the strength of the Chinese Communist government is precisely in the hands of the United States."

U.S. policy makers continue to insist against all the evidence—
slave labor and child labor, persecution of Christians and forced
abortions, closing of markets and theft of intellectual property, sale of
nuclear technology to Pakistan, and shooting of missiles into the
Strait of Taiwan—that China is changing and capitalism is changing
it. Harry Wu describes it very differently:

> The Chinese are operating on several assumptions: that peo-
> ple are more interested in their own economic development
> than in freedom and democracy, that the party can remain in
> power even though communism has failed, that the United
> States and the rest of the industrialized world will pursue eco-
> nomic gain at the expense of human rights in China, and that
> China can expand its military without significant resistance
> from the United States.

My daughters and I attended the 1998 major-league baseball All-
Star game in Denver. As we walked into the ballpark on that warm
July evening, each of us was handed a "special All-Star" Beanie Baby, a
cuddly little red-white-and-blue bear. Affixed to its ear was a "Made
in China" label. We found out later that "only 100,000" of these were
manufactured. Within five steps of the gate, Emily and Elizabeth were

offered fifty dollars each for their Beanie Babies by a young man with a roll of ten- and twenty-dollar bills. A few steps further, long before we got to our seats, another man, with a wad of fifty-dollar notes, offered us one hundred dollars for one of our Made-in-China toys. And after the game, fans leaving the park were offered $125 each to part with their valuable little prizes.

Who made these Beanie Babies? How many days would it have taken the Chinese man or woman—maybe boy or girl—to earn enough to buy one of these Beanie Babies? A month? Three months? At only a few nickels an hour, perhaps six months or a year? And what were the working conditions that produced these Beanie Babies? Were they made by child labor? Or in labor camps? Or were they made by free labor earning twenty-five or thirty cents per hour?

The Chinese Communist Party. The People's Liberation Army. Large, multinational corporations. Which of these want a freer China? Which of these want a China where workers can organize and bargain for better living standards? Which of these will demand human rights for a billion Chinese? Which of these cares about child labor? Which of these *really* wants change?

In the days leading up to the PNTR vote, the plastic phone cards were everywhere. It didn't matter where I was—walking into work, hurrying to committee, even crossing Independence Avenue on the way to vote—an attractive, well-groomed young man or woman thrust a ten-minute phone card in my hand. After dialing the 800 number, the automated voice reminded the caller to ask his or her congressman to vote for PNTR.

Not a bribe, not exactly graft, just a low-cost reminder that commerce always comes first on the floor of the House of Representatives.

6

Myth 6: The North American Free Trade Agreement Has Been a Success

I regret that trade policy has been inextricably linked with job creation. We often try to promote free trade on the mistaken ground, in my judgment, that it will create jobs.

—*Alan Greenspan*

"I am going to continue going forward," Rafael Espinoza said to me in Spanish, all the while looking straight at me. The determination in his face bridged any language barrier. "There is no law that says it's a crime to have a real union. Even if they fire us, we'll continue fighting until we have a union that will wake up and defend our rights under the law."

I spoke with Rafael and Felicia, two autoworkers who are paid about 90 cents an hour, on a warm October day in their ramshackle home in one of the hundreds of *colonias* that have sprung up around Reynosa, Mexico, across the Rio Grande from McAllen, Texas. The NAFTA side agreements, promised by the United States trade representative to deal with labor standards and working conditions, have been of no help to the Espinoza family. Clinton administration negotiators added environmental and labor side agreements after NAFTA was finalized and signed to reduce opposition by Democratic members of Congress. It requires all three countries to enforce their own labor laws, but the mechanisms to enforce the side agreement are weak. A 2001 Human Rights Watch study found that all attempts to use the side agreement to get countries to enforce their own labor laws had failed. They failed in getting independent unions in Mexico and they failed when trying to get the U.S. to enforce its labor laws against apple growers' exploitation of migrant fruit pickers in Washington State.

Indeed, the Espinozas have seen other workers lose their jobs by trying to form an independent union to replace the company-controlled *syndicato,* whose leaders inform on the reformers. "The company says it's losing money, but we know better. They say they have many 'red numbers.' How do you say it? Red ink? But we know they're making a lot of money."

Mexican federal law requires foreign-owned companies to distribute 10 percent of their profits to their workers, but the Espinozas and their coworkers have yet to see a peso of those profits. The Mexican government refuses to enforce its own labor laws. Perhaps they know that United States corporations might sue them under NAFTA, calling the Mexican profit-sharing law an unfair trade practice. Or maybe the Mexican government wants to help U.S. companies save money and encourage more of them to invest in the *maquiladoras.* Either way, General Motors–Mexico, the Espinozas' employer, claims it has no profits from any of its Mexico plants, which are operated as "cost centers" and not "profit centers."

"We need the *maquiladoras* because of our terrible necessity to be working," Rafael continued. "But they are taking advantage of us for their own interests. We know the company doesn't want any bad publicity, so why is there such injustice? Don't the shareholders know about our situation?" He told us how General Motors, the company union, and the government are all arrayed against him and the other workers; they have no ability to demand wages higher than the $40 a week they earn, safer working conditions where an injury underscores how replaceable all of them are, and environmental responsibility, so their children will have safe places to play. Then, with a determination bordering on defiance, he said, "I am not afraid. I am going forward for myself and for my family—for my children. We will not quit."

Things have gotten worse since the 1993 enactment of NAFTA for every family we visited in the Mexican *maquiladoras*. The *maquiladoras* (from *maquilas de oro,* or mills of gold) started with the creation of the Border Industrialization Project in 1965. Export processing zones were established, here and elsewhere, to exploit cheaper labor and tax advantages for the assembly or production of goods that were to be made in one country and shipped to another. The Border Industrialization Project was begun to lure U.S. companies and American investors to seek "their gold" through very favorable tax treatment and other economic considerations by coming to Mexico to build their plants along the United States border. In Tijuana, the busiest *maquiladora* region, the growth of factories has been explosive. From the lone Fairchild Industries plant in 1965, the Tijuana region grew to 94 industrial firms in 1973, 232 in 1986, and about 700 today. Overall in Mexico, there are some 2,800 foreign-owned factories employing more than 1.3 million people, according to the National Association of Maquiladoras. The Mexican government tells us that *maquiladoras* are sometimes organized into Maquiladora Parks. These parks "usually are very nice, with gated entrances and pleasant tree-lined streets and boulevards." The government does not mention in its brochures that Mexican workers, who live almost in the shadow of these factories and tree-lined boulevards, share in almost none of the wealth they create. The workers live in conditions of filth, poverty, and hopelessness only hundreds of yards away from these gated entrances. Many live in cardboard shacks made from packing materials discarded from the plants where they work. Workers at the Whirlpool factory, for example, live in Whirlpool appliance cardboard boxes. The companies rarely pay taxes to the communities in which the *maquiladoras* are located. As a result, the minimum wage *maquiladoras* workers who live in *colonias*—those makeshift communities that have sprung up near the factories—are a tremendous burden on an almost nonexistent infrastructure.

These "mills of gold" attracted little attention from U.S. Congress or the American public until 1986, when President Reagan's Department of Commerce sponsored a seminar in Acapulco to promote U.S. investment in Mexico, especially in the *maquiladoras*. U.S. government officials and trade experts counseled American companies on how to set up manufacturing operations in Mexico, ship finished products back to the United States, and avoid U.S. duties. Predictably, Congress was outraged, but only enough to pass legislation prohibiting the use of public funds for seminars and conferences that urged U.S. companies to invest outside the country. Congress was not sufficiently indignant to actually deal with the burgeoning growth and real problems of the *maquiladoras*.

Journalist William Greider compared the *maquiladoras* with the company steel and coal towns of eastern Kentucky at the turn of the twentieth century: both suffered from low wages, neglect of public investment, dangerous working conditions, degradation of the surrounding environment, and the use of child labor. Kentucky steel and mine workers had no union, the government was always on the side of the owners of capital, and business went virtually unregulated as it influenced the government to do whatever business demanded.

NAFTA supporters, in both Mexico and the United States, promised something very different to the Mexican and American people and to their national legislatures. Congress had granted President George H.W. Bush "fast-track authority" to negotiate the North American Free Trade Agreement with Canada and Mexico. The negotiations were completed and the agreement finalized and signed by President Bush on August 12, 1992; NAFTA would be considered by a new Congress, and managed by a new president.

President Bush's 1991 *Economic Report of the President* summed up how his administration told the country that NAFTA would work. Interestingly, *there is no mention of Mexico as a market for products made in the United States,* inadvertently affirming that NAFTA was about cheap labor and about cutting costs to United States corporations, not about exports and U.S. jobs:

> To reduce costs, companies often allocate phases of a manufacturing process among a number of nations. A free-trade agreement with Mexico would further encourage this *natural* [my emphasis] international division of labor. By lowering the overall costs of U.S. manufacturing firms, a free-trade agreement would make U.S. firms more competitive against imports in the United States and against other countries' exports in the world market. This gain in manufacturing competitiveness *encourages productivity and higher wages* [my emphasis]. The proposed free-trade agreement would similarly boost the competitiveness of Mexican firms. Additionally, the two-way reduction in trade barriers would benefit by supporting its market reforms and encouraging economic growth.

At some point, free trade supporters realized that—contrary to their original claims—they had to sell NAFTA to the American public in a different way; hence, Bush, Clinton, GOP congressional leaders, and U.S. corporations talked about exports and jobs. Under NAFTA, Mexican productivity did go up, but wages dropped precipitously. Wages are 40 percent lower in real terms than they were twenty years ago, in spite of steadily climbing productivity by Mexican workers.

No trade agreement in recent memory had captured the American people's attention the way that NAFTA did. During the 1992 presidential election, President Bush actively campaigned for the agreement that his administration had negotiated. Candidate Clinton, whom Bush thought he had put in a political no-win situation because of Clinton's anti-NAFTA labor support and pro-NAFTA high-tech business support, wiggled out of it by conditioning his support for NAFTA on its including labor and environment side agreements—that is, enforceable labor standards for Mexican workers and meaningful environmental safeguards built into Mexican law. Self-financed Independent candidate Ross Perot was a strong opponent of NAFTA, and warned repeatedly that the trade agreement would hemorrhage thousands of U.S. jobs.

In July 1993 President Clinton's negotiators announced they had arrived at an agreement on labor and the environment. Negotiated almost as an afterthought to allay the fears of environmentalists and labor unions, it satisfied no one. Most observers thought the agreement was not particularly substantive, and most NAFTA supporters found it not especially bothersome. Most of us who were opposed to the agreement found the side agreements virtually meaningless. It was clear to us by then that if labor standards and environmental rules were not in the core agreement, they were simply unenforceable.

Proponents insisted upon hasty passage of the agreement. If Congress did not act quickly, they predicted, investors would lose confidence in Mexico, the stock market in that country would collapse, America would lose its export edge, and the peso would plunge. If Congress did not move, Europe and especially east Asia would invest in Mexico at our expense. In the end, Congress did act quickly . . . and all the dire predictions happened!

Responding to investor warnings and intense business and political pressures, Congress passed NAFTA in less than a year, even though probably a majority of the majority Democrats wanted to consider and pass health care first. Other Democrats wrote the president asking him to work with them to pass welfare reform before we took up NAFTA, but House Speaker Thomas Foley (D-Washington State) believed that hasty passage was necessary to preclude the doomsday warnings served us by the administration and business leaders in Mexico and the United States.

Supporters of NAFTA argued that the long-term economic benefits would outweigh the short-term costs of minor job loss, although many NAFTA proponents would not even acknowledge short-term job loss. In the end, hundreds of thousands of jobs would be created, they promised. President Bush's NAFTA advisers had predicted an almost immediate gain of more than 200,000 U.S. jobs. By eliminating tariffs—a border tax, in effect—on products coming to and from Canada, Mexico, and the United States, more goods and services would flow among the three countries, creating jobs and more prosperity in all three nations. Before NAFTA, the average tariff on Mexican goods sold into the United States was 4 percent, while tariffs on American goods sold in Mexico averaged 10 percent. The agreement eliminated tariffs on almost ten thousand products over a fifteen-year period. Eliminating all duties would thereby supposedly create more advantage—and more jobs—for the people of the United States.

More prosperity in Mexico, NAFTA supporters contended, would

mean higher wages, a stronger Mexican middle class with greater buying power, and a cleaner environment that only a wealthier Mexico
would be able to afford. The trade surplus of $6 billion in the early
1990s that America enjoyed with Mexico would grow and mean more
benefits for the United States as the Mexican middle class expanded,
NAFTA optimists argued. USA NAFTA, a group made up of America's
largest corporations, called NAFTA "the best international trade
agreement" the United States had ever signed. The always somber
Henry Kissinger, who represents international businesses that benefit
from free trade, weighed in as well. Dramatizing the moment,
Kissinger, afflicted with terminal importance, endorsed NAFTA with
great solemnity: "About once in a generation, this country has an opportunity in foreign policy to do something defining, something that
establishes the structure for decades to come."

Furthermore, Mexico, with more than 90 million people just
south of our border, was moving toward democracy, supporters assured us. Its president, Harvard-educated Carlos Salinas de Gortari,
had a very solid reputation among the American business and diplomatic elite. His dress and his English were impeccable (better, in both
cases, than some members of Congress, we were told), and his advisers and assistants were Mexico's "best and brightest." President
Clinton's secretary of the treasury, Lloyd Bentsen, when asked why
Congress should pass NAFTA, replied, "One word. And it's spelled
S-A-L-I-N-A-S."

A lot of us—Mexicans and Americans—had a very different
image of Salinas. Never a democrat, and never a believer in equal opportunity, the Mexican leader wanted to rein in the democratic forces
in his country. "Salinas created NAFTA as a reaction to democratiza-
tion, to control it," Lorenzo Meyer of the Center for International
Studies of El Colegio di Mexico told me on a December day in 2003.

"Salinas wanted a China way out," Meyer said. He was looking for a China-style Mexican government, authoritarianism with economic liberalization. As the leader of the ruling party, the PRI, which had governed Mexico for almost seventy-five years, Salinas had presided over an economy where riches were shared by very few, a government where corruption ran rampant, and a police force where dissent was not tolerated. Privatization of government enterprises had enriched many of Salinas's friends beyond their imagination. After the passage of NAFTA and after his term expired, Salinas joined the board of Dow Jones—only one month after the collapse of the Mexican peso. His brother Raul, a midlevel government bureaucrat, was discovered to have stashed tens of millions of dollars in Swiss, German, British, and U.S. bank accounts—money made, it was believed, by drug trafficking while his brother was president of Mexico. In January 1999 Raul was convicted of murder and sent to prison for his role in the 1994 assassination of a PRI rival. The former Mexican president himself later fled abroad—nobody was quite sure where—as more stories of his and his brother's corruption came to light. He later settled in Ireland, and eventually returned to Mexico.

There was little improvement in human rights, in spite of NAFTA promises, in the years after its approval. Of all our major trading partners, Mexico is the most prominent one cited for torture by the United States Department of State. Between 1989 and 1997, 562 members of the PRD opposition party had been murdered. The Inter-American Press Association lists Colombia—where the United States is involved in a drug war—and Mexico as the two nations in this hemisphere where the most journalists have been killed or attacked during the past decade. The Organization of American States cited Mexico's continually rising rate, post-NAFTA, of forced disappearances and illegal detentions. Amnesty International noted that there were as many as one hundred forced disappearances in 1997 in the state of Chihuahua alone.

NAFTA opponents had very different predictions from those of USA NAFTA, Salinas, and Kissinger. Unless there were solid core agreements on minimum wage, worker safety, democratic reforms, and the environment, there would never be a middle class in Mexico, opponents contended. NAFTA would simply lock in an exploitive political and economic system. It would also mean movement of high-paying jobs south to low-wage Mexico. With its very weak environment and labor side agreements, NAFTA would help neither the people of Mexico nor the people of the United States. "It was negotiated," Michigan Democrat David Bonior said on the House floor as he and I discussed NAFTA during a Special Order speech, "purely in the interest of multimillionaire investors and multinational corporations, at the expense of working people and their families on both sides of the border."

Those investors, multinational corporations, and the Mexican elite were certainly not shy about preparing to take advantage of NAFTA. The Mexican state of Yucatan ran full-page advertisements in American trade magazines beckoning U.S. businesses to journey south: "You can't cut labor costs 300% [sic] in 90 minutes," says a concerned Anglo businessman. "Yes you can in Yucatan . . . and you can save over $15,000 a year, per worker." And another ad shows a worried North American scratching his head: "I can't find good, loyal workers for a dollar an hour within a thousand miles of here. . . ." "Yes you can in Yucatan. . . . and you could save over $15,000 a year, per worker."

NAFTA opponents were also concerned that the rush to pass NAFTA was concealing a perilously weak Mexican peso. Small Business Committee chairman John LaFalce, a Buffalo Democrat, held hearings on the potential problems of the weak Mexican peso and what might happen if the peso were devalued. Economist Jeff Faux presciently wrote:

> There is the risk of integrating Mexican financial institutions, regulated by a corrupt one-party regime, with an already fragile U.S. financial system. NAFTA makes it much easier for U.S. banks, security firms, and so on, to buy into Mexican industry. This creates the possibility that when the next debt crisis hits, the U.S. government will have to rescue the Mexican economy in order to protect major American banks.

In July 1993 I made a speech to the Cleveland City Club calling for a side agreement on currency stabilization. Neither a dismissive press nor a single-minded administration took it seriously. The media were too busy writing and talking about Ross Perot's belief that there would be a "giant sucking sound of jobs going to Mexico" to bother with the more complex issues of potential peso devaluation and the development of export platforms.

There is a NAFTA we could have supported, a fair-trade agreement rather than a free-trade agreement. The slogan adopted by many of the grassroots opponents to the agreement was "Not this NAFTA," an indication that we wanted an agreement which raised living standards in Mexico instead of lowering them in the United States, and which emphasized social justice, respect for the environment, and local empowerment. Provisions for free-trade unionism, labor standards that include worker safety and a minimum wage, peso devaluation, environmental rules, food safety, and building in democratic guarantees and building up democratic institutions would have turned many NAFTA opponents into enthusiastic supporters. The agreement could have required all three countries to meet the strictest labor standards found in any of the countries, and unions and workers could have been given the right to challenge any import that was made in violation of the country's labor standard. These standards—environment, food safety, labor—could have been enforced through trade sanctions.

The distinguished Mexican academician and future foreign minister Jorge Castañeda called for an agreement that:

> includes compensatory financing, encourages industrial planning and a common regulatory framework, confronts the issue of worker mobility, harmonizes upward labor standards and rights, creates an environmental and consumer protection charter, and institutes a broad multi-purpose dispute-resolution mechanism.

Instead, the North American Free Trade Agreement included none of these provisions. By any measurement, NAFTA has failed the American people—in trade balance, health and food safety, truck safety, illegal drugs containment, environment, and agriculture.

U.S. Trade Balance

Although American politicians and business leaders have been ominously quiet about the effects of NAFTA on the U.S. economy, they have, when asked, trumpeted facts and figures about the increase in U.S. exports to Mexico. Free-trade proponents almost never discuss the net effect of trade flows—the trade balance—because the United States increasingly imports more than it exports. In 1997 the Commerce Department proudly proclaimed that Mexico was now the second-largest purchaser of U.S. goods, and in the summer of 1998, United States Trade Representative Charlene Barshefsky told *World*

Trade, a magazine devoted to free trade, that "If we look at 1996 to 1997, our exports to Mexico are up 26 percent in that year. They are at record levels, all-time highs." In a 1999 "NAFTA Turns Five Years Old" article that neglected to talk about trade deficits, *Newsday* reported only that "trade between Mexico and the United States [has soared] from $80 billion a year pre-NAFTA to an estimated $200 billion in 1998."

But that doesn't come close to telling the real story. The destination of virtually the entire increase of U.S. exports to Mexico has been the *maquiladoras,* the region along the border where foreign investors have located to produce goods for export to the United States. And these exports are overwhelmingly factory components to build new plants or parts to be assembled for exports. Rarely are they consumer goods.

Here's how it works. After the November 1993 passage of NAFTA, more and more American companies made the decision to erect factories in northern Mexico, along the Rio Grande in the *maquiladoras.* To build these plants, the contractors needed machines and tools and equipment. As the plants were constructed, these one-time exports went to Mexico, building an infrastructure and creating a path for manufacturing jobs to go from the United States to Mexico. All these goods count on the trade ledger as American exports, even though they were helping these companies take jobs to Mexico.

The second and larger type of U.S. exports to Mexico was what economist and trade expert Harley Shaiken terms "industrial tourists." These component exports, visiting Mexico for only a few days, stay in Mexico just long enough to be assembled in the *maquiladoras,* from which the finished product is shipped back to the United States. These "industrial tourists," often auto parts, for example, stay in Mexico about as long as a San Diego teenager visiting Tijuana. And it is not just manufactured components that make the trip south. Only 2 percent of raw materials purchased by *maquiladora* plants in 1997 came from Mexican suppliers; most came from the United States. Such "industrial tourists" still count as exports from the United States to Mexico. If a plant in Brownsville, Texas, moves to Matamoras, Mexico, its U.S. suppliers contribute to U.S. exports to Mexico. These revolving door "exports" have accounted for the entire export increase for the United States. In 1993, the year before NAFTA went into effect, the U.S. sold to Mexico $27.1 billion in final exports, goods that were actually consumed in Mexico. The next year, that number increased to $28.5 billion. In 1995 it dropped to $19.7, and 1996 it climbed to $25.9. More telling perhaps were the temporary exports, those components that directly replace American jobs; they were the biggest gainers—from $18.2 billion in 1993 to $41.7 billion in 1996. More concisely, in 1993 more than 60 percent of U.S. exports to Mexico were final exports. In 1996 only 38 percent were. By 2002 the share of final exports was up but was still only half of all exports to Mexico. Only 32 percent of our imports from Mexico were *not* from firms operating in Mexico.

The other side of the export equation is even more revealing. While U.S. exports, about which our trade officials brag so proudly, have grown, at least on the temporary side, our imports from Mexico have skyrocketed. Mark Levinson, chief economist of the Union of Needle Trades, Industrial and Textile Employees, told *Newsday,* "What the administration does is it says U.S. exports to Mexico are up, therefore more jobs must have been created. That's like saying the Yankees are playing the Red Sox and the Yankees scored eight runs. Great. But they don't tell you that the Red Sox scored fourteen. Telling you about imports without talking about exports is like giving half a score in baseball." *

---

* *Anyone* outscoring the Yankees is a good thing!

Our trade balance with Mexico, which was a $1.7 billion trade surplus in 1993, went into deficit the first year of NAFTA in 1993, and ballooned to a $14.7 billion deficit in 1998, $17 billion in 2000, $37 billion in 2002, and almost $50 billion in 2005. Our trade deficit with Canada jumped to $18.5 billion in 1998, $19 billion in 2000, $48 billion in 2002, and $70 billion in 2005.

United States Manufacturing Jobs

Before NAFTA, Mexico was America's only major trading partner with whom it had a surplus. Economists who supported NAFTA calculated that a $1 billion trade surplus or deficit translates into about 20,000 jobs, generally good-paying industrial jobs. The Bush and Clinton Department of Commerce, historically free trade's strongest advocate in the president's cabinet, also calculated 13,000 jobs per $1 billion net deficit or surplus. Net American job loss from the North American Free Trade Agreement, under traditional economics calculation, far exceeded 1,000,000 jobs.

Public Citizen surveyed American companies who promised job increases during their lobbying efforts for NAFTA; fully 90 percent of those jobs never materialized. The only real job growth in those American companies, to no one's surprise, was south of the border—at about one-fifteenth the wages. Using a narrow definition, the U.S. Department of Labor certified that 525,000 jobs were lost because of NAFTA between 1994 and 2002. The Economic Policy Institute in Washington, D.C., used a more careful econometric analysis to determine that the United States lost nearly 800,000 jobs between 1994 and 2001 as a result of NAFTA. And that was before the huge manufacturing jobs losses of the George W. Bush years.

While the U.S. economy obviously did well in the 1990s, growth in the domestic auto industry was weaker. Mexican auto exports to the United States doubled from 1993–1996. We now buy almost one million vehicles from Mexico, manufactured mostly by east Asian and American auto companies. Mexico buys fewer than 100,000 vehicles from the United States. The auto deficit has risen to over $15 billion. The cumulative U.S. NAFTA vehicle deficit with Mexico between 1994 and 2005 exceeded $120 billion.

The American textile and apparel industries have done worse. In response to congressional requests during the NAFTA debate, the United States International Trade Commission projected that there would be some job loss and increase in U.S. imports: "Removal of U.S. quotas and tariffs will likely result in an increase in U.S. apparel imports from Mexico of roughly 45 percent in the short term and 57 percent in the long term. . . . The expected changes in U.S. textile and apparel trade under NAFTA will likely have a minor positive impact on production and employment in the U.S. textile industry and a minor negative impact on production and employment in the U.S. apparel industry. . . . Even if U.S. apparel imports from Mexico grow by as much as 200 percent in the long term, the U.S. industry's labor force will likely decline by about 3 percent." But, as with almost all NAFTA predictions from supporters of the agreement, the damage was far, far underestimated. Apparel imports from Mexico increased in the first five years of NAFTA by 475 percent, and, as economist Mark Levinson pointed out, failing to calculate the effects of capital mobility, quota elimination, and currency exchange, average annual employment in the apparel industry declined 6.6 percent annually in the first five years that NAFTA was in effect. The five years prior to the agreement saw annual declines of only 1.6 percent.

Some of the biggest beneficiaries of NAFTA have been those who actually wrote the rules. Two principal negotiators (one a Mexican economist, the other an American businessman) of the apparel and textile sectors of the trade agreement have established a joint venture called NuStart, which has helped set up an industrial park where 8,000 people will eventually work. The joint venture plans to develop about a dozen more. Those who work there are paid about $3.25 a day.

The National Textile Industry Chamber of Mexico expects apparel companies to spend $1.2 billion over the next two years in capital improvements and construction. And textiles by necessity will eventually follow apparel. Guilford, Burlington, and Parkdale—all North Carolina mills—are spending several hundred million dollars on Mexican textile mills so that the fabric will be manufactured closer to the sewing.

None of this should have come as a surprise. A *Wall Street Journal* survey of U.S. corporate executives prior to the NAFTA vote in 1993 found that 40 percent had plans to move at least some of their production to Mexico. Fully a quarter of them admitted that they were going to use the threat of moving as a bargaining tool with their employees to cut wages and benefits.

Economic Damage to Mexico

The greatest damage to Mexico from NAFTA has come from the worsening wage and productivity gap. The minimum wage in Mexico, when it is enforced, is about four dollars a day. Twenty years ago, in real purchasing power, it was literally three times that. Since 1993, when NAFTA was enacted, productivity of Mexican workers has steadily climbed, while wages, especially after the huge peso devaluation, have dropped sharply. For most workers, that translates into a 50 percent decline in their standard of living.

The most compelling selling point of NAFTA was its promise to create wealth and a strong middle class in Mexico, which could then produce more jobs, and provide people with the disposable income needed to join the consumer society. It would mean a more prosperous neighbor to the south, more exports and jobs for U.S. companies, and less illegal immigration from Mexico to the United States because economic opportunity in Mexico would blossom. Yet between 1993 and 1996, productivity in Mexican manufacturing rose 38 percent while hourly wages for production workers *fell* by 21 percent. By 1996, three years after NAFTA's enactment, the hourly manufacturing wage in Mexico was still only one-tenth that of the United States. "The single biggest flaw in the North American Free Trade Agreement," Minority Leader Richard Gephardt wrote to Democratic members of Congress in 1996, "was its failure to adequately address industrial relations—the right to strike, the right to organize, and the right to freely associate." As a result, wages did not keep up with productivity.

Since the International Monetary Fund's bailout after the peso devaluation, 25,000 small Mexican firms have gone out of business, two million workers have lost their jobs, and wages have plummeted 40 percent. Mexico has become a poorer country, as NAFTA's promises have been left unfulfilled. The *Wall Street Journal* admitted that the peso devaluation and the resulting Mexican bailout caused Mexican living standards to drop by a full 50 percent. In 1981, 49 percent of Mexicans lived in poverty. The 2000 Mexican census showed that 75 percent lived in poverty after seven years of NAFTA. Literally one-half of the country, some 50 million people, according to a study by the National Autonomous University in Mexico, are "extremely poor," compared to 31 percent in 1993. Eight million more Mexicans have fallen into poverty since the passage of the North American Free Trade Agreement.

As already mentioned, among Mexico's working class, salaries fell

40 percent from 1994 to 1997, and statistics from the United States Department of Labor show that the hourly wages of Mexican industrial workers are only 9.6 percent of the wages earned by United States industrial workers, down from 22 percent in 1980. Prior to the 1970s, Mexican workers earned one-third the wages of Americans, according to economist and former Mexican senator Rosalbina Garavito. Conditions were considerably worse in the *maquiladoras*. Workers in these modern, often high-tech plants, almost all owned by foreigners, were paid one-third less than those in older Mexican plants in the country's interior, yet the lower-paid workers' productivity was much, much higher, and the differential between pay and productivity was growing every year.

More often than not, Mexican *maquiladora* autoworkers live in squalor in the shadow of the plants where they are creating great wealth for their owners. They build a shining city, yet live in a city dump only a few hundred yards away. Usually they have no electricity in their rundown shacks, no running water, no sewage disposal. Mexican employees run machines powered by electricity yet often have no electricity at home to run a stove. *Maquiladora* workers use hundreds of gallons of purified water to run complicated, high-tech manufacturing processes, yet in most cases they have no running water to wash their hands at home and no clean water to drink. The auto plants have no employee parking lots because their workers cannot afford to buy the products that they make. The workers are rarely allowed, beyond subsistence living, to share in the bounty that they have created with the sweat of their brows and the work of their hands.

How can Mexico become a consumer market for U.S. exports with a minimum wage of less than four dollars a day? How can the promises of NAFTA be fulfilled when workers cannot buy what they make? It is hardly a prescription to build a consumer society and create a vibrant middle class. Yet some did very, very well. While Mexican wages—both inside and outside the *maquiladoras,* but especially inside—were declining, U.S. companies in Mexico were increasing sales back into the United States by almost two and a half times. Auto exports to the United States from Mexico were seven times the sales of autos from the United States to Mexico. So, while workers in the United States lost jobs, American CEOs who brought industrial plants to Mexico often did very well, taking in huge profits from their Mexican operations, and leaving little behind for Mexican workers. The chief executive officer for Allied Signal, for example, was paid 50 percent more than his company's 3,800 *maquiladora* workers combined!

American border towns, expecting a gushing stream of Mexican citizens to visit their communities with their newfound wealth, have been sorely disappointed. The *Wall Street Journal* in August 1998 chronicled the disappointment with NAFTA in American town after American town along the Mexican border. The population of Nogales, Mexico, thanks to American investment in that community's *maquiladoras,* has doubled in five years, while Nogales, Arizona, its sister city on the border, has seen its population stagnate and its unemployment rise to 23 percent. Almost half of the downtown stores are boarded up, and sales tax receipts have dropped 20 percent in the five years of NAFTA. The peso devaluation, coupled with the abysmally low and declining wages in the *maquiladoras,* has made Arizona prices too high for Mexicans.

In the much larger city of El Paso, Texas, across the Rio Grande from Ciudad Juárez, Mexico, the news on the American side of the border is no better. Sixty stores closed there after NAFTA was enacted. Ten thousand jobs have moved south, mostly to its sister city. Most of these jobs are in the apparel industry, where U.S. companies pay five or six dollars an hour, while *maquiladora* companies—most of them American-owned—a few hundred yards away pay five dollars a day.

El Paso's unemployment rate climbed to twice the national average. Capital can move easily; people cannot.

NAFTA supporters like to blame Mexican workers' conditions on the huge peso devaluation, as if their trade agreement had nothing to do with the peso's collapse. But Mexico's history speaks otherwise. Its lack of democracy and democratic institutions like labor unions have locked in an exploitive situation which has delinked productivity and wages. Listen to the words of Abraham Lincoln: "The strongest bond of human sympathy, outside of the family relation, should be on uniting all working people, of all nations and tongues and kindreds." From 1980 to 1993 manufacturing productivity rose 53 percent while real wages were 30 percent lower. Workers worked harder, better, and more productively, yet they realized few of the gains from their labors. Even in the first year of NAFTA, before the peso bailout, manufacturing productivity rose 10 percent while wages went up only 3 percent. The leadership of the trade union movement, co-opted by business and the government, collaborated with the government to keep wages down. In fact, the nonunion/union wage differential—large in democracies with free-trade unions—went from 25 percent in 1984 to an almost imperceptible 3.5 percent in 1996.

Much of the problem of low wages centered on "collective protection contracts," Antonio Villalba Granados told me one day in the summer of 1999 in my Washington, D.C., office. A member of the Frente Autentico del Trabajo (Front of Authentic Workers) for thirty years, he pointed out that company-friendly unions, encouraged by the government, sign contracts that have very low wages and few or no benefits. Workers often do not even know there is a union. Jesus Campos Linas, a Mexican labor lawyer, said, "The government uses these labor federations to get votes during elections. Companies make hefty regular payments to union leaders under these contracts and, in return, get labor peace."

As government policy has weakened unions, business and government policy makers are trying to do much more. As Mercedes Gema López Limón, professor at the University of Baja California in Mexicala, told David Bacon, associate editor of the Pacific News Service, "Our government and corporations are using privatization to do away with unions entirely." Thirty years ago, 75 percent of Mexicans belonged to a trade union; today fewer than one-third do. At PEMEX, the state-owned oil company, more than 70 percent of workers belong to a union, but in the once similarly constructed petrochemical industry that has been privatized over the last fifteen years, less than 10 percent now belong to a union.

Unfortunately, complained independent Mexican senator Adolfo Aquilar Zinser, who later became Mexico's ambassador to the United Nations, "We became partners in trade with only a business agenda. We never adopted a political agenda." Consistently low wages in Mexico—under an oppressive NAFTA that locked in a plutocratic, corrupt government—will never allow Mexican workers to become middle-class consumers. NAFTA dictates to the Mexican people only a "dead-end development strategy," in the words of economist Thea Lee: attracting foreign investment with low wages, unenforced worker safety laws, nonexistent environmental rules, and weak and co-opted labor unions. As U.S. multinational corporations locate in Mexico, the number of available workers—because of high birthrates and migration from southern Mexico where peasant corn farmers have been displaced—continues to outstrip the number of jobs, helping to keep wages low. The minimum wage, and logically the average wage, have dropped precipitously since 1980, with an even larger plunge after the enactment of NAFTA.

Health and Food Safety

Michigan Democrat Bart Stupak had presciently told us, during a 1993 special order, that NAFTA would likely affect ownership and use of Great Lakes water. Nothing, of course, was more important to our region of the country than this huge body of water: for drinking water, recreation, commerce, and manufacturing. Stupak—who represents a district bordering Lake Superior, Lake Michigan, and Lake Huron—had quickly established himself as an expert on Great Lakes issues. As he predicted, some years later a company attempted to buy billions of gallons of Great Lakes water to ship to Asia, which over time would have dropped lake levels by as much as several inches. Although various levels of government were able to stop the sale, the impact of NAFTA on lake commerce was becoming more apparent.

That became more clear to me in November 2005, when I was sitting in the Toledo office of Dan Smith, vice president of the American Maritime Officers Union. "When the lake drops even one or two inches," he told me, "ships carry less cargo" because of the navigability of the rivers feeding into the Great Lakes.

Although the side agreements negotiated by United States Trade Representative Mickey Kantor in 1993 before NAFTA's passage required the United States to spend $1.5 billion on environmental cleanup along the border, not one dime had been spent in the agreement's first three years, and only a few dollars have been spent since. To add insult to injury for these depressed American border cities, congestion on both sides of the border is almost unbearable, as "industrial tourists" go south and finished products go north. Chemical spills from trucks going and coming from the border crossing have forced Nogales, Arizona, to spend $300,000 to set up its first hazardous waste team. Air pollution from Mexico is so bothersome that Douglas, Arizona, offered to pave the dirt streets of neighboring Agua Prieta, Mexico. And significant amounts of groundwater contamination come from leakage from aging, deteriorating pipes on the Mexican side.

Along the border, in Mexico as well as in Texas, New Mexico, Arizona, and California, tuberculosis and hepatitis rates have doubled, and in some cases quintupled. Ciudad Juárez, for example, has no sewage treatment plant. With the increasing population in that city since NAFTA, tons and tons of sewage are going into the Rio Grande and making children sick on both sides of the border down the river. The Texas Department of Health disclosed that, since 1993 when NAFTA took effect, the incidence of hepatitis A in Cameron County increased almost 400 percent; in Maverick County it more than doubled, and in Webb County it increased 78 percent. The neural tube defect rate for babies born in Cameron County, Texas, is almost double the national average. The American Medical Association has called the border areas a "cesspool of infectious diseases."

At first, no one could figure it out. In March 1997 a couple dozen children at Hughes Elementary School in Marshall, Michigan, left school with intense stomach pains. Over the next several days, 153 children and teachers at Hughes and other area schools were diagnosed with hepatitis A. Several were hospitalized. Lindsay Doneth, a normally healthy ten-year-old girl, was one of the most seriously ill. On day one, her mother, Sue Doneth, told me, Lindsay complained of body aches and headaches. The second day, she vomited and seemed to have the flu. The next day, she curled up in a ball on the couch and "held her stomach, sobbing in pain." On day four, her parents took her to the emergency room at the local hospital, where she remained for eight days, continually vomiting. She was hooked up to an IV, which delivered painkilling medication and antinausea drugs, and desperately needed fluid. It had to be something in the school cafeteria, local authorities finally figured. Frozen strawberries had been mislabeled as produced in America. Part of the federal government's school lunch program, they had come from Mexico a year earlier, and then were processed and frozen by San Diego–based Andrews and Williamson.

It is illegal to use foreign-grown produce in federally administered school lunch programs. Fred Williamson, the president of Andrews and Williamson, resigned almost immediately. The Food and Drug Administration told Congress that the strawberry fields in Mexico were located next to open privies.

Dr. David Johnson, chief medical executive with the Public Health Agency of the Michigan Department of Community Health, said that thousands of students, teachers, administrators, support staff, and parents at about 350 schools might have been exposed to the Hepatitis A virus; many showed no symptoms. The incubation period of the virus is typically fifteen to fifty days.

Children in six states may have been exposed to the virus, although no other cases were reported. But 9,000 California schoolchildren and 2,000 in Georgia were inoculated after the Michigan outbreak. The Florida Agriculture Commissioner ordered some 105,000 pounds of Mexican strawberries to be pulled from the shelves in his state's schools, partly because of safety and health issues and partly because the violation of federal school lunch law displaced fruit that Florida's growers could have sold to these schools.

Agricultural imports from Canada have increased 300 percent, and from Mexico imports have increased by more than 83 percent from 1994 through 2002, yet the sponsors and supporters of NAFTA have failed to keep up. During this period, while more than half of our fruit and vegetable imports come from Canada and Mexico, Food and Drug Administration inspections have declined from 8 percent of imports to less than 2 percent. The FDA has inspected and tested even fewer products for harmful bacteria, viruses, or parasites. Not to be outdone by the U.S. substandard performance on ensuring food quality, Mexico slashed its spending on food safety from $25 million in 1992 to $5 million in 1995.

There are no requirements in NAFTA for any signatory country to maintain a minimum level of food safety. In fact, Section 717 forbids any special, more rigorous inspections of Mexican produce when it comes across the border, even though imported strawberries from Mexico were found to have an 18.4 percent violation rate for illegal levels of pesticides.

The United States has bilateral agreements with every country in the Western Hemisphere from which it imports beef and poultry. Those agreements allow U.S. Department of Agriculture inspectors to visit the sites where cattle and poultry are raised, and where the slaughtered animals are processed. We do not, however, have similar arrangements for fruits and vegetables; the Food and Drug Administration, the federal agency that inspects for microbial contaminants on fruits and vegetables, has no authority to inspect produce outside the borders of the United States. Legislation which Michigan Democrat John Dingell and I wrote in 2002, however, gives the FDA the authority and better technology to inspect and detain food at the border, to debar importers who have brought adulterated food into the United States, and to require food importers to provide more documentation about growing and processing conditions and country of origin. Nonetheless, tests at the border for microbial contaminants and pesticide residue often take as long as several days or even a couple of weeks to obtain results, and there are no reliable tests for some parasites and viruses that might contaminate food. Some significant parts of our bill were included in the 2003 bioterrorism law (PL107-188), but the legislation fell far short of ensuring that our food supply is as safe as possible.

A report to President Clinton released in May 1998 on food safety prepared by the Department of Health and Human Services, the Department of Agriculture, and the Environmental Protection Agency pointed out how unprepared we are. While food imports have sharply risen, FDA food inspections have precipitously dropped from 21,000 in 1981 to 5,000 in 1997. While our leaders—notably presidents of both parties and the Republican leadership of the House of Representatives and the Senate—have been so strongly committed to free trade and open borders, they have failed to appropriate the money necessary to ensure the purity of our food. The huge budget deficits, coupled with President Bush's request in 2004 and 2005 for further tax cuts, make the outlook for more comprehensive food inspection even bleaker. An earlier report, three years after the trade agreement with Mexico and Canada had been enacted, found that agriculture imports under NAFTA had overwhelmed the ability of the Agricultural Marketing Service to carry out its legal responsibility to regulate commodity imports. The inspector general at the Department of Agriculture found:

> The Agricultural Marketing Service has been unable to perform all required inspections of imported fruits and vegetables to be sold in retail markets. Over 3.7 million pounds of Mexican raisins and olives did not receive inspections. Over 695,000 pounds of lower-grade potatoes that should have been used only for processed food were instead distributed in supermarkets as fresh. Streamlined rules to speed entry for importers were abused to avoid required inspections.

Caroline Smith DeWaal, director of food safety at the Center for Science in the Public Interest, said, "We've got a lot of fruits and vegetables imported from countries where we're warned not to eat them raw or drink the water. The question is, why is it safe to eat it when it's imported?"

The problems of food safety—poor sanitation, weak laws, and poor enforcement of food safety standards in many Latin American countries from which we import; inability of American FDA officials to inspect foreign food producers' facilities; and far too few inspections at the border by U.S. officials, all in the face of a cascading of food imports into the United States—are compounded by our trade laws. Pesticides banned in the United States—nuarmiol, prothiophos, butachlor, to name only a few—are in many cases still manufactured by American chemical companies and exported to developing countries with less stringent environmental and worker safety laws. These chemicals, often carcinogenic, are sprayed onto fields and find their way back to the United States as residue on fruits and vegetables. Nuarmiol, manufactured by Dowelanco, was banned in the United States because it was found to be carcinogenic and teratogenic (causing fetal abnormality) in animals. A fungicide used on bananas, it is exported to Columbia and Honduras for use on their banana plantations. Prothiophos, also not used in the United States, is exported by Mobay, its manufacturer, to the Bahamas, El Salvador, Honduras, and Costa Rica. It was banned in the United States because it was found to be a cholinesterase inhibitor in fish, highly toxic to fish and birds, and poisonous to humans in some situations. Latin American farmers use this insecticide on grapes, pears, and most frequently on bananas. Although butachlor is banned in the United States because it causes serious alterations in the environment, fauna, and fish, this pesticide is used on paddy rice that is then imported into the United States. Monsanto exports butachlor to Argentina, Brazil, Venezuela, Uruguay, Paraguay, Peru, Ecuador, Columbia, Panama, Costa Rica, Guatemala, and Honduras. Yet NAFTA and other trade agreements have failed to address the issue of pesticide export. A better NAFTA would have helped Latin American farmers who are now exposed to these toxic substances, Latin American consumers who eat the produce, and American consumers who buy the imported foods.

The goal of trade negotiators is to harmonize health and safety standards as trade flows more and more freely across national boundaries. Harmonization—bringing standards together, ultimately making them identical—almost always means lowering the standards in the country which has the strongest environmental, worker-rights, and food safety laws. Harmonization fits perfectly the agenda for American agribusiness, chemical companies, and other U.S. firms that have for years battled the federal government's Environmental Protection Agency and Occupational Safety and Health Administration.

As the Bush administration has worked overtime to weaken environmental and food safety rules in the United States, Bush trade negotiators are trying to do the same in the global economy: Let the marketplace determine and construct the global economic structure, free traders insist. Unregulated global commerce will lower our production costs, they add, and help our productivity.

There is every economic incentive to lower cost and to weaken health and safety standards. Firms, left to themselves, will almost always lower costs by externalizing pollution control, worker safety, and health-care costs—that is, by letting society bear those costs instead of the manufacturer who produced them. Why pay for disposal of toxic wastes if your competitor is not, and if government does not require it? And why stay in a nation or move to a country where there are laws that require your business to internalize those costs? The lack of international laws for environmental protection, for example, encourages firms to go to the nation with the weakest standards. Unregulated international commerce, a global economy with no democratic controls, encourages industry to shift its production to the nations with the fewest requirements, the weakest laws, and the lowest costs. These nations are rarely democracies; that's why harmonization always translates into weaker standards.

Environment

Prior to the enactment of NAFTA, only governments were permitted to sue other governments; no trade agreement had ever allowed private concerns to sue foreign governments. Trade agreements before NAFTA prohibited the parties from collecting monetary damages; the penalty for the losing nation was to have its tariff removed or to allow the other country to impose a tariff against the offending nation. But under NAFTA, a corporation—a private, for-profit company—can sue a foreign government and collect damages against the taxpayers of that sovereign, democratic nation.

Under NAFTA's Chapter 11, which took effect in 1996, more than a dozen challenges have been brought against nations, demanding damage payments of more than $1 billion. Six of those challenges have come from U.S. corporations against the governments of Mexico or Canada. Three of them are lawsuits to force the opening of hazardous waste disposal facilities in Mexico.

Five years earlier, Canadian author Margaret Atwood, who referred to her dominant neighbor to the south as "the great star-spangled Them," had warned her countrymen about NAFTA: "I believe the free-trade issue has the potential to fragment and destroy the country in a way that nothing else has succeeded in doing." She was, as many Canadians are, afraid of a further integration of Canada's and America's economies, cultures, and ways of life. In an essay about NAFTA, Atwood wrote:

As George Bernard Shaw commented when a beautiful actress wanted to have a child with him so it would have her looks and his brains, "But madam—what if it has my looks and your brains?"

We'd like to think we're about to get the best of both worlds—Canadian stability and a more caring society, plus American markets—but what if instead we get their crime rate, health programs and gun laws, and they get our markets, or what's left of them?

People in Canada are beginning to see, unfortunately, that she was all too prescient.

In many cases, American environmental standards are not the strictest of the three countries. Ethyl Corporation, located in Richmond, Virginia, used NAFTA against the Canadian government to undermine one of Canada's most important clean air laws. Founded eight decades ago by General Motors, DuPont, and Standard Oil, the Ethyl Corporation produces a lead additive to gasoline to improve the fuel's performance. When the United States Environmental Protection Agency banned the use of lead in gasoline in the 1970s, Ethyl developed and began to sell methylcyclopentadienyl manganese tricarbonyl (MMT) as a fuel additive to improve gasoline performance. MMT is a manganese-based compound that, when added to gasoline, enhances octane and reduces engine "knocking." Manganese has long been known to be a neurotoxin at high doses when inhaled, raising a warning flag about its potential to cause health effects at lower doses (which have never been adequately studied). In June 1998 the American Medical Association's House of Delegates expressed concern about "long-term, low-dose exposures to MMT and its combustion products, particularly effects on vulnerable populations."

MMT is banned in California, and the U.S. Environmental Protection Agency has prohibited its use in reformulated gasoline, the fuel that is used in most major metropolitan areas. It is legal, but almost never sold, in other areas of the United States. In addition, automobile manufacturers contend that MMT damages pollution control equipment in vehicles, which in turn means more emissions, and more pollution.

In early 1997 when the Canadian Parliament was debating a ban on MMT, Ethyl lobbied against the ban, arguing the product's safety and threatening a lawsuit if the Parliament passed the bill. The Canadian Parliament enacted the ban anyway in early April, and the Ethyl Corporation filed a lawsuit against the Canadian government on April 14. Citing the NAFTA prohibition on "expropriation" of property (taking another's property for oneself), and using the newly created power for private corporations to sue sovereign, elected governments, Ethyl claimed that the ban "expropriated" their property, causing lost sales and profits and harm to its reputation. With "private legal standing" granted to it in Chapter 11 of the North American Free Trade Agreement, the Ethyl Corporation asked for $251 million in damages, in part because Canada hurt Ethyl's "good reputation." Ethyl was operating under the assumption that Canada was in violation of NAFTA because the trade agreement was supposed to harmonize environmental standards, generally to the lowest common denominator, and almost always to the benefit of business and to the disadvantage of public health and the environment.

Fearing it would lose the MMT lawsuit, the Canadian government settled with the Ethyl Corporation. An angry Canadian environmental and public health community was shocked at the way NAFTA worked against them and against the public interest, and how a U.S. company had so directly intervened in Canadian politics. Nonetheless, as part of the agreement with Ethyl Corporation, the

Canadian government lifted the ban on MMT and agreed to pay the Virginia company $13 million (U.S.) in damages for lost profits.

American citizens have equal reason to feel wronged by Chapter 11 of NAFTA. MTBE is a carcinogenic gasoline additive banned by the state of California because it leaked into the groundwater at Lake Tahoe and into 10,000 wells in that state; in July 1999 the United States Environmental Protection Agency stated that the use of MTBE should be "reduced substantially" because it dissolves easily in water and turns up in tap water when gasoline has leaked or spilled. The Methanex Corporation of Canada, the manufacturer of MTBE, reacted by suing the United States government for $1 billion in lost *and future* profits. The California ban, and the legislation introduced in Congress in 1999 which would ban MTBE nationwide, had caused a precipitous drop in the company's stock prices, according to Methanex counsel. In August 2005 a NAFTA tribunal dismissed Methanex's billion-dollar claim against the United States. The tribunal found that California did not expropriate Methanex property. Public Citizen's Trade Watch wrote, "The Methanex case is among the 42 cases filed by corporate interests and investors under NAFTA's Chapter 11 investor provisions. With only 12 of the 42 cases finalized, some $35 million in taxpayer funds have been granted to five corporations that have succeeded with their claims. An additional $28 billion has been claimed by investors in all three NAFTA nations. Seven additional cases against the United States are currently in active arbitration." Opponents of these kinds of regulatory clauses contend, rightly, that domestic laws or trade agreements which allow for takings would either bankrupt government or force repeal of all kinds of health and safety regulations.

A central part of the 2001 congressional debate on President George W. Bush's request for Trade Promotion Authority evolved around Chapter 11. Many of us in Congress fear extending Chapter 11–type provisions to another trade agreement, shifting more power to corporations, further undercutting public health laws enacted by democratic governments. What happens next? As power shifts from governments to corporations, surely other companies will follow the lead of the Ethyl Corporation and the Methanex Corporation, attempting to strike down environmental laws, food safety regulations, and consumer protection statutes. The Ethyl Corporation's lawsuit and Canada's decision to settle suggest that when one country's public health laws collide with another country's private corporation's profits, the public's right to environmental protection might be in jeopardy. Business opponents of strong environmental regulations may have found a strategy to weaken environmental laws in all three countries.

As we explore the environmental problems along the border, it is important to remember that Mexican law requires that imported hazardous materials, of which tons cross the border every day, must be shipped back to the United States. But, according to journalist William Greider, researchers found that only 5 percent of the hazardous materials could actually be accounted for in U.S. Customs Department documentation. They suspect, but cannot prove, that most of the toxic waste is trucked to illegal dumps in the interior of Mexico, "future Superfund sites," Greider writes, "waiting to be discovered by Mexican authorities."

Agriculture

NAFTA has not worked for small farmers north or south of the Rio Grande. NAFTA required the revocation of decades-old land reforms, which had made it difficult for large U.S. companies to purchase large tracts of land. With inexpensive land, cheap labor, and the liberal use of many chemicals banned in the United States, these corporate farms produced tomatoes that were imported without tariffs into the United States at a price cheaper than Florida-grown tomatoes. In NAFTA's first five years, more than one hundred Florida tomato farmers went out of business, two dozen packing houses closed, and hundreds more suppliers and processors shut down. Interestingly, imports of Mexican tomatoes have increased 70 percent, while, according to the Department of Labor's Bureau of Labor Statistics, consumer prices for tomatoes have increased 16 percent in the United States. So much for imports bringing prices down.

Mexican corn farmers, on the other hand, tell a different but equally tragic, story. In the poor, very rural, southern Mexican state of Chiapas, in the aftermath of the enactment of NAFTA, thousands of peasants were pushed off the land that their families had farmed for dozens of generations. Their primitive methods of farming—which had sustained them and their families for hundreds and hundreds of years—could not compete with large, efficient, highly mechanized farmers in Kansas, Iowa, Illinois, and Ohio, especially when U.S. farmers benefited from government subsidies. On one October 2003 morning at the Capitol, John Audley of the Carnegie Endowment for International Peace explained to a group of congressmen why Mexican farmers could not compete with American agribusiness: Much of the corn grown in the United States for sale to Mexico, he told us, is grown in some of the most arid areas with the help of major irrigation efforts. "Essentially," he said, "they are packing water in the form of corn and exporting it to Mexico." The Institute for Agriculture and Trade Policy in Minneapolis pointed out that U.S. corn sells for 25 percent less in Mexico than its true cost. Mexican farmers claim that they lose money for every ear of corn they sell. More than 1.7 million jobs have been lost in the Mexican countryside.

Almost immediately after the passage of NAFTA, American farmers began to capture Mexican markets, making it impossible for Mexican peasants in places like Chiapas to sell their corn and earn a living. Nearly one million Mexican farmers have been displaced, many of whom head north in search of job opportunities in America. And it is getting worse. According to Tina Rosenberg of the *New York Times,* European farmers now get 35 percent of their income from government subsidies, and American farmers got 20 percent. Those subsidies have made life ever more difficult for many of the 18 million Mexicans who live on small farms. Baldemar Velásquez, a long-time farm-worker organizer in Toledo, Ohio, who began work in the fields at the age of six, told me that there are a large number of workers from Chiapas who are harvesting pickles (cucumbers) in northwest Ohio, 1,800 miles from their ancestral home.

Rafael Espinoza, on that October morning, told me he needed his *maquiladoras* job. At least, he said, he's making some money to support his family, meager though the support is. "But we need some rules in the same way that you and your government have rules for your workers—for safety at our jobs, for better wages, for us to be able to join a real union, one that's on our side. But we don't have much hope," he said wistfully, "that the Mexican government will ever help us."

Rafael's cousins to the south have no idea what's in store for them. Neither do the citizens of the United States. Negotiations on the Free Trade Act of the Americas (FTAA) began in 1994, the same year that the North American Free Trade Agreement went into effect. The talks involve 34 countries representing 800 million people—twice the size of NAFTA with four times the number of low-wage workers. Until recently, the trade ministers had hoped to conclude negotiations, push the agreement through their national legislative bodies, and put the hemispheric economic blueprint into effect by 2005; but widespread opposition, especially from Venezuela and Brazil, have rendered the outcome in doubt.

And they don't want anyone to know about it. The draft language has mostly been kept out of public view. In July 2001, 435 pages of the draft text were released, but it was largely unintelligible because much of it was bracketed, or struck out from public view. Public interest groups have had no access to the talks, while at least 500 corporate representatives have had security clearance. Citizen groups that have demanded access have begun to compare the talks to Vice President Cheney's success in writing the Bush administration's energy bill behind closed doors. Others have noticed the similarities between these secret negotiations and the House-Senate conference committee on the Medicare bill. To be sure, Ambassador Zoellick has learned something from his Republican brethren in Washington.

The picture is this: government officials and corporations are writing a blueprint to govern an economy of 800 million people. It will affect manufacturing, the environment, food safety, financial services, health care delivery, and every other part of our economic lives. And it reaches far beyond any previous trade agreement. Former trade representative Charlene Barshefsky bragged in 1999, "However ambitious the WTO is, the FTAA by definition is significantly more ambitious."

For years, experts on both sides of trade issues have pronounced that the impending trade agreement for the entire hemisphere would be based on a NAFTA model. Only in the last few months have we seen that FTAA is much, much worse than the North American Free Trade Agreement and the World Trade Organization. That's why the battle in Congress over FTAA will dwarf the fight on NAFTA in 1993, PNTR in 1999, and CAFTA in 2005, mainly because the WTO is limited to trade issues but has not expanded to investment issues. FTAA proposes the elimination of barriers to both goods and services. While NAFTA included side agreements—albeit weak ones—on labor rights and the environment, FTAA will not. Even worse, governments would be forced to prove that their public health and clean air and water standards are both "necessary" and "least trade restrictive." The challenges are directed by unelected trade bureaucrats; the burden of proof falls on democratically elected governments.

If NAFTA is an economic constitution for Mexico, Canada, and the United States, FTAA is a bill of rights for the Western Hemisphere's corporations.

7

Myth 7: Free Trade Is a
Great American Tradition

So convenient a thing it is to be a rational creature, since it enables us
to find or make a reason for everything one has a mind to.

—*Ben Franklin*

On November 9, 1993, Vice President Al Gore hit a home run for free trade. In the nationally televised NAFTA debate with Texas billionaire and former presidential candidate Ross Perot, the vice president scored big. Producing photographs of the late senator Reed Smoot (R-Utah) and the late congressman Willis Hawley (R-Oregon), Gore claimed that their tariff legislation passed in 1930 had been the "principal cause of the Great Depression." Perot stared into the camera, stammering, and had nothing to say.

It was an impressive debate point for Gore, to be sure—except the vice president had the facts wrong. But he was in good company. That fall, the *Wall Street Journal* could hardly contain itself in its support of a position by a Democratic administration: Smoot-Hawley "represented a brand of dumb and reactionary Republicanism that consigned the party to also-ran oblivion from 1932 through Robert Taft." Six years later, during a trade skirmish between the United States and the European Union, the *Wall Street Journal* excoriated that same free-trade administration, screeching that it wasn't free-trade enough and accusing it of "leading the charge toward the same kind of protectionist chain reaction that with the Smoot-Hawley tariff in the early 1930s severely curtailed world trade and contributed importantly to the Depression and, ultimately, World War II."

Free trader Ronald Reagan had ridiculed Smoot-Hawley several times during his presidency: "Smoot-Hawley helped bring on the Great Depression, making it virtually impossible for anyone to sell anything in America. . . . It brought about the collapse of the world trading system." He warned against a "trade war, a war we fought in 1930 with the infamous Smoot-Hawley tariffs and lost." And *Business Week* opined, "The Smoot-Hawley tariffs paved the way for World War II."

The *Economic Report of the President* in 1988 told us the same thing:

> The lesson of Smoot-Hawley is that passage of protectionist legislation by the United States will increase protectionist activities in the rest of the world, poison the international climate for trade diplomacy in general, and slow the process for trade liberalization for years to come. Since the United States is a major trading nation, it could suffer major economic losses in the event of increased global protectionism.

When senator-elect Reed Smoot came to Washington in early 1903, he of course expected to take his seat in the United States Senate. A practicing Mormon, he immediately became caught up in a swirl of controversy. Accused of polygamy, which was at that time still permitted in his church, and of other illegal activities under U.S. law, the Utah Republican was refused his seat. It was not until four years later, in February 1907, that he was allowed to actually join the Senate. He later became chairman of the Senate Finance Committee, under whose jurisdiction tax laws and tariffs fall. After he left the Senate, he became one of twelve apostles of the Church of Jesus Christ of Latter Day Saints and, at the time of his death in 1941, was third in line to succeed the president of the church.

The route to Washington was a bit easier for Willis Hawley, who came to Congress from Oregon's 2nd district in 1906. As chairman of the House Ways and Means Committee in the late 1920s and early 1930s, Hawley presided over the tariff controversy in the House. To write the tariff legislation, he created fifteen subcommittees of three members each, knowing of course that home-state interests would win out when considering duties on all kinds of potential imports.

In June 1930 President Herbert Hoover signed the Smoot-Hawley Act, which raised tariffs for 20,000 items. Eight months earlier the stock market had crashed, and American corporations had lost one-tenth of their value. By early summer of 1930, 10 percent of Americans had lost their jobs, banks were shutting down, people's savings were lost, and factories were closing. Even though the United States enjoyed a trade surplus, the majority in Congress believed that selective tariff increases could help to stanch the gushing of the nation's economic blood. At the time, few blamed the new tariff law for the stock market crash or the depression.

But critics have had a field day since: they have asserted that Smoot-Hawley caused the stock market crash and the Great Depression; that Smoot-Hawley provoked major retaliation from our largest trading partners all over the world; that Smoot-Hawley gave us the highest tariff schedule in American history.

Former chairman of the United States International Trade Commission and now Ohio University historian Alfred Eckes assails those ill-informed politicians, economists, business leaders, political opportunists, and editorial writers who raise the straw man of Smoot-Hawley while knowing little about it: "That the legend of Smoot-Hawley endures and continues to influence trade policy debate is a tribute to the public relations skills of partisans and ideologues with agendas. They successfully transformed a molehill into a mountain."

The myths of Smoot-Hawley do not withstand the light of day:

The stock market crashed on October 29, 1929;
Smoot-Hawley did not pass until June 1930.

The stock market reached its lowest point on November 13, 1929, when it fell to 198.69. By the following April, when a tariff bill appeared imminent, the market had rebounded to 294. Even though the market dropped several points the week that the president signed the bill, most analysts at the time believed that Wall Street was responding to newspaper editorials about foreign retaliation, little of which materialized. By mid-July, the market had recovered almost all of its lost ground.

There is no evidence that Smoot-Hawley either caused
or deepened the Great Depression.

After the stock market crash of October 1929 and the weakening of the American economy, consumer purchases—imports and domestically produced goods alike—began to slow significantly as people's buying power plummeted. One might expect that, after the passage of Smoot-Hawley, those goods with high duties would experience more significant declines than those goods with no import duties. But that did not happen. According to historian Eckes, imports of dutiable and nondutiable goods each declined 52 percent. And even more significantly, from 1932–1936, as the economy began to recover, the value of high-duty imports climbed at a faster rate (136 percent) than duty-free imports (56 percent).

Politicians and journalists typically overestimate the impact of tariffs and trade on a nation's economy as a whole. At the time of enactment of Smoot-Hawley, total imports accounted for about 4 percent of the nation's Gross National Product. Dutiable goods—remember, fully two-thirds of all imports were duty-free—made up only 1.3 percent of America's GNP. Is it conceivable, presidential candidate Pat Buchanan asked, "that an increase in tariffs on 1.3 percent of the GNP triggered the collapse of five thousand banks, wiped out five-sixths of the stock market, caused a drop of 46 percent of the GNP, and sent unemployment soaring to 25 percent?"

Smoot-Hawley was decidedly not the highest tariff schedule in American history.

Two-thirds of our nation's imports after Smoot-Hawley were duty-free, a number that has since declined to about 35 percent. The number of duty-free imports under Smoot-Hawley was the largest in American history. The average duty on all imports called for under the 1930 act—dutiable and nondutiable combined—was 13.7 percent, a proportion lower than each of the 94 preceding years. The tariff on dutiable imports was significantly higher, 44.7 percent, which was lower than many preceding years but higher than the post–World War I years. Nonetheless, tariffs were clearly not the highest in American history, not even the highest in the twentieth century. In fact, a bipartisan Congress enacted higher tariff schedules in 1932, two years after Smoot-Hawley, on selected energy and mining commodities. Furthermore, during the 1932 elections, President Hoover and the Republican Congress asked the United States Tariff Commission for higher tariffs to protect specific U.S. industries and farm groups.

While retaliation might have been expected when a country with a trade surplus increases its tariffs, only four countries lodged formal diplomatic complaints against the United States.

To be sure, the worldwide depression caused many nations to enact higher tariffs to protect their industries and their jobs, but that wave of protectionist legislative impulses began before the enactment of Smoot-Hawley. Several European nations levied tariffs after World War I, a dozen years before Smoot-Hawley, to protect those industries that had suffered during the war. But major retaliation seemed hard to find. Canada, the country most heavily and directly affected by U.S. trade actions, lodged no complaint. The secretary of the British Board of Trade allowed that he had little "doubt whether trade as a whole has been so little affected as the parties particularly injured are inclined to suppose." The Department of State circulated a Tariff Commission questionnaire to American embassies around the world inquiring about trade retaliation against the United States. The State Department then reported, "With the exception of discriminations in France, the extent of discrimination against American commerce is very slight. . . . By far the largest number of countries do not discriminate against the commerce of the United States in any way."

The anger aimed at the United States for its enactment of Smoot-Hawley centered around the fact that Congress raised the tariffs of a nation that was already enjoying a persistent and significant trade surplus. Exports had exceeded imports for thirty-four years in a row. A deficit country was not enacting protectionist measures; a surplus country was. Imagine if Japan had raised its tariffs in the 1980s; there would have been an international outcry. It is simply very difficult, in the court of international public opinion, for a country with a large trade surplus to justify hiking its trade tariffs. In that context, but in that context *only*, Smoot-Hawley deserved the criticism that was leveled against it in the early 1930s.

The same editorial writers, free-trade advocates, politicians, and business leaders who have for seven decades so successfully spun the Smoot-Hawley myth tell us that America always supported free trade and kept our tariffs low, that our business titans and government officials urged others to do likewise, and that we prospered as a result. The facts tell a very different story.

In the eighteenth century, it was clear to U.S. policy makers that our future well-being depended on building up an industrial base, often subsidizing our nation's producers, and protecting our industries by tariffs from cheaper and more sophisticated foreign competition. Students of history in developing countries know that just about every wealthy, industrialized nation on earth followed similar paths in their development. Government and business usually worked hand in hand to bring prosperity to a new, developing nation. France and Germany followed that course. So have Japan and Taiwan and Korea. And so did the United States.

Germany in the nineteenth century industrialized by shepherding its resources, protecting its industry, and foregoing purchases of oftentimes desirable foreign goods. France and most other modern, industrialized nations understood that their well-being as nations depended on developing their industrial base, protecting their workers and manufacturers, building up their education system, and often subsidizing their production. Economic nationalism worked in Taiwan, South Korea, Japan, Singapore, and Hong Kong—countries with free markets but with protectionist, managed-trade policies. As

South Korean economist Jene Kwon pointed out, the industries that grew the fastest were those subsidized and overseen by the government. Those countries and economies did best when governments and banks, often nationalized, developed strategies, targeted industries, and restricted foreign investment. As trade expert John Judis also pointed out, "Subsidies were granted to business—but only in exchange for meeting specific performance requirements. And planners placed a high priority on becoming competitive through higher productivity rather than through lower wages."

"The project of economic expansion," wrote historian Arthur Schlesinger Jr. in *Cycles of American History*, "based on internal improvements, tariff protection, the Bank and land legislation, soon acquired a name—the American system." Yet in recent years, private investors in the United States—and a government that is especially responsive to those private investors—have used America's lucrative market, global diplomatic leverage, and financial power to move developing countries in a very different direction from the one we pursued.

With the United States, it started early. As a member of Congress, Abraham Lincoln believed that a tariff protected jobs and served as a significant raiser of revenue—a tax on those who were willing to pay it by buying foreign items. "Give us a protective tariff, and we will have the greatest country on earth." In his days as a Whig, during the 1844 elections, Lincoln wrote:

> Those whose pride, whose abundance of means, prompt them to spurn the manufactures of our own country, and to strut in British cloaks, and coats, and pantaloons, may have to pay a few cents more on the yard for the cloth that makes them. A terrible evil, truly to the Illinois farmer, who never

wore, or expects to wear, a single yard of British goods in his whole life.

After his nomination as a candidate for president in 1860, Lincoln described himself as "a Henry-Clay-tariff-man." The Morrill Tariff was considered by many to be Lincoln's greatest prewar achievement. His beliefs were unequivocal:

> I don't know much about the tariff. But I know this much. When we buy manufactured goods abroad, we get the goods and the foreigner gets the money. When we buy the manufactured goods at home, we get both the goods and the money.

Through the last century and a half, prominent Americans understood that tariffs could be useful, and that cooperation between government and industry could help to build a strong and livable nation. As chairman of the House Ways and Means Committee, which wrote trade laws, and as president, Ohio's William McKinley always believed in the use of tariffs to protect the public interest:

> Open competition between high-paid American labor and poorly paid European labor will either drive out of existence American industry or lower American wages. [Protectionism] has made the lives of the masses of our countrymen sweeter and brighter, and has entered the homes of America carrying comfort and cheer and courage.

His successor, Teddy Roosevelt, who became president after McKinley's 1901 assassination, was also a supporter of tariffs and what they could do for the American economy. In 1895, Roosevelt wrote: "Thank God I am not a free trader," adding that "pernicious indulgence in the doctrine of free trade seems inevitably to produce fatty degeneration of the moral fiber." And he understood that industrial policy and tariffs could pay dividends for the nation.

Many in the United States have forgotten how the U.S. government used market intervention, subsidies for favored industries, and tariff protection for its manufacturers. Editorial after editorial in America's leading newspapers today preach how the United States is a nation based on free trade, that our history is a shining example of free markets open to the wares of the world, and that our unregulated global commerce has brought us prosperity for over a hundred years. But U.S. history paints a very different picture. America forgets, as Robert Kuttner tells us:

> There is now a sharp distinction between the policy the U.S. pursued for most of its first two hundred years, and the advice it now proffers to today's developing economies. Most emergent nations have in fact followed the developmental path of the early United States, using state power to blend technical learning and economic development with a tolerable measure of sovereignty. But in recent years, the U.S. government and American private investors have used America's significant global diplomatic leverage to move emergent economies onto a path very different from our own: to promote entry for foreign private capital, ban discrimination in favor of domestic production, and turn away from public investment, public regulation, public subsidy, and public ownership.

Japan and all of east Asia have practiced trade according to their national interest for decades, something Americans have never quite figured out. They do not think they have cheated when they find loop-holes to keep American products out while aggressively selling their products into our market. The government has simply done what it thinks best for the country and its citizens. Export-led growth economies work when only a relative few, generally smaller, countries play the game—or when one really large country with a huge, lucrative market is willing to absorb billions and billions of dollars of exports. The United States has played that role for years, and seems eager to continue to play it well into the next century, but in the end, an export-led economy for east Asian nations and a pliant, some would say gullible, import-fed U.S. will not be good for either partner.

Most of the world's successful economies—Japan and the Four Tigers (Singapore, Taiwan, South Korea, and Hong Kong), Europe, and the United States—pursued a policy of protection for their industry, government, and business partnerships, incentives for investment and research, and support and subsidies for public utilities and key industries. We tell developing countries around the world that they must cut government spending, weaken their infrastructure, slash corporate taxes, privatize public utilities, limit production to only one or two major commodities, charge user fees to the poor, spend less on education and health care, and grant expanded rights to foreign investors—all so they can build export-driven economies. No matter that their debt, in many cases, is twice their Gross Domestic Product. Even free-trade enthusiast Paul Krugman, an economist and columnist for the *New York Times,* acknowledged, "Policy makers in Washington and bankers in New York often seem to prescribe for other countries the kind of root-canal economics that we would never tolerate here in the U.S.A." Do as we say, not as we did, we seem to be telling them.

For 200 years, as Robert Kuttner recounts in *Everything for Sale,* we built our nation by blending state power with technical learning and economic development. The young nation—from the Northwest Ordinance to the Small Business Administration—combined the power and resources of the government with the entrepreneurial talents of its people. Land grant universities and government-assisted research discovered information and created jobs in the private sector. Taxpayer-subsidized railroads, airports, and the interstate highway system helped private businesses form and expand. Partnerships among business, government, and schools built our economy. The strength of labor unions created and expanded a huge middle class. And the involvement of civic organizations helped to provide a cohesion that pulled us together. Neither foreign powers nor international investors, unlike in the global economy today, had much influence on our economy or our way of life.

But we now tell developing countries to abandon the American model of development, the path we took to prosperity. Our Africa policy is a good example of the hypocrisy of U.S. behavior. Stalled twice in Congress but finally passed in the spring of 2000, the African Growth and Opportunity Act (referred to by opponents as the "NAFTA for Africa bill"), in some sense, was much more insidious than NAFTA. It contained all the negative elements of NAFTA but it went further. Any African nation that wanted to take advantage of the provisions of the bill had to follow the economic course laid out by the conservative congressional authors of the bill, something even NAFTA never did.

In other words, to qualify for admission into the agreement and to gain access to the U.S. market, each African nation would have to pursue an aggressive privatization of its economy and a laissez-faire agenda. Slash government spending, Republican Ways and Means bill writers paternalistically and knowingly tell Africa, if you want to be part of this legislation. Weaken environmental standards and worker rights if you want access to wealthy American consumers. Charge user fees to the poorest of the poor, in many cases, for health care and education. Then cut education and infrastructure expenditures if you want access to the most lucrative market in the history of the world— all things that we as a nation, in the early years of our development, did not do because we were a democracy, because no foreign power wielded great influence over us, and because, over time, we had strong labor unions and a pluralistic democracy that insisted collectively on labor standards and environmental and public health protections.

Take but one example. By loaning the Congo more than a billion dollars many years ago for a power line to facilitate exports, even though most economists knew it was not practical, the World Bank assured a huge, unmanageable debt that can only be repaid—over many, many years, if at all—by sales of Congo cobalt and diamonds. As a fictional Leah pronounced in Barbara Kingsolver's novel, *The Poisonwood Bible,* "With a foreign debt now in the billions, any hope that was left for our Independence is handcuffed in debtor's prison."

The sponsors of the African Growth and Opportunity Act repeatedly told us that Africans wanted this bill, that it was Africa's big opportunity to raise its standard of living and to participate in the global economy as a major player. Most of Africa's leaders endorsed it. A letter cosigned by almost every African ambassador to the United States landed on the desk of every member of Congress extolling the virtues of the African Growth and Opportunity Act. It seemed that everyone in Africa was for it.

Not so fast, insisted Jean Bakole, international coordinator for the African Organization's Coalition for Food Security, Trade, and Sustainable Development. "The African people have not spoken with you," he told Congresswoman Barbara Lee (D-Oakland), Congressman Jesse Jackson Jr. (D-Chicago), and me one day in Jackson's office.

"You only hear from the governments and the diplomatic corps."
South African president Nelson Mandela was also critical of the legis-
lation: "This is a matter over which we have serious reservations. . . .
To us this is not acceptable."

In Seattle in December 1999 at the meeting of the World Trade
Organization, we heard the same arguments from developing countries' prime ministers, finance ministers, and ambassadors. "People
in our country do not want labor standards," Asmat Kamaludin,
secretary-general of the Ministry of International Trade and Industry
of Malaysia, told me in a private meeting in a barricaded Seattle hotel.
He and Ambassador Dato Ghazzali Sheikh Abdul Khalid pointed out
to Congressman Sandy Levin (D-Michigan) and me that raising
wages and enacting and enforcing workers' rights would destroy their
economy. When pressed, however, both admitted that union leaders
and union members in Malaysia did in fact think labor standards
were a good idea. It was the same everywhere. The leaders of most developing nations—drawn almost exclusively from the countries'
wealthiest families—almost always supported trade agreements with
no environmental and labor standards. It is no different from the domestic agenda advocated by George W. Bush and the wealthy families
in the United States as they pursue policies to weaken domestic environmental and labor standards in their own country.

But many people in their countries saw things much differently. A
joint statement signed by almost 1,000 labor, environmental, consumer, church, and development groups, representing seventy countries mostly from the Third World, opposed a new round of the
World Trade Organization, believing labor standards would become
even more difficult to attain. *American Prospect* reported that a former U.S. State Department official said at a meeting of the Council on
Foreign Relations: "What you don't understand is that when we negotiate economic agreements with these poorer countries, we are nego-

tiating with people from the same class. That is, people whose interests are like ours—on the side of capital."

While the elite in Africa might benefit from the African Growth and Opportunity Act, as the elite in Mexico benefit from NAFTA, tens of millions of working-class Africans would not. African trade union leaders—from groups as disparate as the Zimbabwe Congress of Trade Unions to COSATU, the giant South Africa labor union federation—understood that the future well-being of their nation depends on educating its people, learning how to make steel, how to manufacture its own products, how to build roads.

In early 1999, partially in response to the African Growth and Opportunity Act, Congressman Jackson Jr. introduced H.R. 722, the Human Rights, Opportunity, Partnership, and Empowerment (HOPE) for Africa Act. It set labor standards, minimum wages, and environmental rules for trade between the United States and sub-Saharan Africa. The bill stipulated that any business enterprise must comply "with the environmental standards that would apply to a similar operation in the United States, the European Union, Japan, or any other developed country (or group of developed countries), as the case may be." We as sponsors believed that Jackson's bill, unlike NAFTA for Africa, would help to create a middle class in Africa, would result in higher wages, would empower workers, and would raise Africa's standard of living.

No nation forced an austerity on the United States or on a developing France or Japan, or even on a growing South Korea or Taiwan, which could have choked economic development. No foreign nation demanded of England or Canada an export economy to become eligible for trading privileges. No outside force required cuts in education spending or a tearing of the social safety net that weakened the formation of a middle class.

The myth of the sanctity of free markets and free trade began 150 years before Smoot-Hawley. Twentieth-century free traders extol the virtues of Adam Smith's* oft-cited invisible hand in the domestic marketplace and apply those same principles to the international global economy. But Smith, citing the "vile maxim of the masters of mankind," understood the power of the employer in the workplace in the domestic and international economy: "People of the same trade seldom meet together, even for merriment and diversion, but the conversation ends in a conspiracy against the public, or in some contrivance to raise prices." He understood the conflict between large business and the public interest:

> It is the industry which is carried on for the benefit of the rich and the powerful, that is principally encouraged by our mercantile system. That which is carried on for the benefit of the poor and the indigent, is too often, either neglected, or oppressed.

He warned against child labor, too many hours in the workday, and "excessive application" of work by the employer. Since history began, Smith observed, while the invisible hand has brought efficiency to economic systems, it also can wreak havoc on the less advantaged, the ill-educated, the vulnerable, and the unlucky. And all too often, Smith noted, the "masters themselves" use the government that they can almost always influence to wring additional advantage out of the working classes. In *The Nature and Causes of the Wealth of Nations,* Smith also wrote about industrial England:

---

* As far as I could tell in reading Smith's 1776 masterpiece, *The Nature and Causes of the Wealth of Nations,* Smith used the term "invisible hand" only once in his most famous book.

It is not difficult to foresee which of the two parties must, upon all ordinary occasions, have the advantage in the dispute, and force the other into compliance with their terms. The masters, being fewer in number, can combine much more easily, and the law does not prohibit their combinations, while it prohibits those of the workmen. We have no acts of Parliament against combining to lower the price [wages] of work, but many against combining to raise it.

Smith's warnings went unheeded. Parliament banned any associations among workers to bargain for higher wages, fewer working hours, or better working conditions. Governments colluded with employers against workers almost everywhere. Says Smith, "The obstruction which corporation laws give to the free circulation of labor is common, I believe, to every part of Europe." Smith's invisible hand, paradoxically with the government's help, played the role for "the vile maxim of the masters of mankind." He wrote of "the natural combination of masters not to raise wages."

Smith would recognize the masters today, not the "merchants and manufacturers" of eighteenth-century Britain but the large multinational corporations and the gargantuan financial houses which move their capital from country to country, searching for the cheapest labor with the lowest environmental and worker safety costs. In Smith's day, they were the "principal architects" of the state's behavior—because of their influence in the parliaments of European democracies and in the courts of European autocracies. Today, they are little different, and their reach is global. They are the *maquiladora* employers who meet monthly to plot strategy to keep unions weak, wages down, and troublemakers out. They are the wealthiest families of Indonesia who rule the country and conspire with Western multinational corporations, generating huge profits for the families themselves and for Western investors. They are corporate executives from the United States who lobby Congress for Permanent Normal Trade Relations for China, representing their own interests and the interests of the Chinese Communist Party and the People's Liberation Army at the same time. They are the World Bank and the International Monetary Fund that always know best.

Sometimes it is clear that the World Bank and the IMF do not know best. Former Haitian president Jean-Bertram Aristide tells a story of the power and influence—and bad judgment—of these international institutions:

> The eradication of the Haitian Creole pig population in the 1980s is a classic parable of globalization. Haiti's small, black, Creole pigs were at the heart of the peasant economy. An extremely hearty breed, well adapted to Haiti's climate and conditions, they ate readily available waste products, and could survive for three days without food. Eighty to 85 percent of rural households raised pigs; they played a key role in maintaining the fertility of the soil and instituted the primary savings bank of the peasant population. Traditionally, a pig was sold to pay for emergencies and special occasions (funerals, marriages, illnesses), and, critically, to pay school fees and buy books for the children when school opened each year in October.
>
> In 1982, international agencies assured Haiti's peasants their pigs were sick and had to be killed (so that the illness would not spread to countries to the north). Promises were made that better pigs would replace the sick pigs. With an efficiency not since seen among development projects, all of the Creole pigs were killed over a period of 13 months.

Two years later, the new, "better" pigs came from Iowa. They were so much better they required clean drinking water (unavailable to 80 percent of the population), imported feed ($90 a year when the per capita income was about $130), and special roofed pigpens. Haitian peasants quickly dubbed them "prince a quatre pieds," (four-footed princes). Adding insult to injury, the meat didn't taste as good.

Needless to say, the repopulation program was a complete failure. One observer of the process estimated that in monetary terms, Haitian peasants lost $600 million. There was a 30 percent drop in enrollment in rural schools, a dramatic decline in the protein consumption in rural Haiti, a devastating decapitalization of the peasant economy, and an incalculable negative impact on Haiti's soil and agricultural productivity. Haiti's peasantry has not recovered to this day.

Most of rural Haiti is still isolated from global markets, so for many peasants the extermination of the Creole pigs was their first experience of globalization. The experience looms large in the collective memory. Today, when the peasants are told that "economic reform" and privatization will benefit them, they are understandably wary. The state-owned enterprises are sick, we are told, and must be privatized. The peasants shake their heads and remember the Creole pigs.

Heralded as perhaps history's greatest proponent of capitalism, Adam Smith more often than not sided with workers. Contrary to the teachings of his twentieth- and twenty-first-century apostles, he was oftentimes supportive of government intervention—especially when the object is to reduce poverty: "When the regulation, therefore, is in support of the workman, it is always just and equitable; but it is sometimes otherwise when in favour of the masters." The distinguished American economist John Kenneth Galbraith said about *The Wealth of Nations,* "It is much celebrated by the ministry of the righteous right, few of whom have read it. Were they to do so—disapproval of the corporate form, approval of a wealth tax—they would be greatly shocked." Or, as conservative Edward Luttwak, senior fellow at the Center for Strategic and International Studies, wrote in his 1999 book *Turbo Capitalism: Winners and Losers in the Global Economy:* "The god of the market-worshippers . . . is Adam Smith, but theirs is a devotion that depends crucially on not reading him. Being far wiser than his modern worshippers, Smith filled his work with exceptions, exclusions, and reservations to the rule that free markets always allocate most efficiently, maximizing the common welfare."

Throughout his life, Smith recognized and understood the goals of the elite: The elite's interest, he wrote in *The Wealth of Nations:*

> In any particular branch of trade or manufactures, is always in some respects different from, and even opposite to, that of the public. . . . The proposal of any new law, or regulation of commerce, which comes from this order, ought always to be listened to with great precaution and ought never to be adopted . . . but with the most suspicious affection. It comes from an order of men . . . whose interest is never exactly the same with that of the public, who have generally an interest to deceive, and even to oppress, the public and who accordingly have, upon many occasions, both deceived and oppressed it.

He advocated high wages as beneficial to employer and employee alike, and advocated the abolition of slavery because "the work done by free men comes cheaper in the end than that performed by slaves," not so much because of a fear of revolt but because generally satisfied well-paid workers would create wealth in a society, and increase purchasing power for the domestic economy: "No society can surely be flourishing and happy, of which the far greater part of the members are poor and miserable. It is but equity, besides, that they who feed, clothe, and lodge the whole body of the people, should have such a share of the produce of their own labour as to be themselves tolerably well fed, clothed, and lodged." Smith intuitively understood that higher wages meant a stronger middle class, with more commerce and trade among all classes, and a more stable society. Workers would be able to buy the products they made; they would share in the wealth they create.

Smith's support of free trade seemed contingent on several things: He supported the Acts of Trade and Navigation, requiring British goods to be sent on British ships manned by British sailors. He believed that tariffs serve a useful purpose. He expressed caution when a nation contemplates lowering tariffs, for an immediate and precipitous reduction could throw large numbers of people out of work. And he expressed little caution about retaliatory tariffs when one nation has erected major barriers against another to harm that nation: "The recovery of a great foreign market will generally more than compensate the transitory inconveniency of paying dearer during a short time for some sorts of goods," he wrote. Economic historians and less learned editorial writers seem to have forgotten that Smith, in foreign trade as in the domestic economy, believed that his invisible hand could do great harm to a nation and its citizens "unless government takes great pains to prevent it."

Two hundred years later, Adam Smith's invisible hand would guide an economy driven by consumer behavior, occasionally regulated by government, and measured by its consumption and ever-growing standard of living. Low prices mattered. Comparative advantage—British economist David Ricardo's theory by which the lowest-cost producer should produce and sell—mattered. The buyer always stood paramount. And society's success was a product of the degree and quantity of purchase. But neither Smith nor Ricardo foresaw the mobility of capital; they expected capital to remain in the home country while goods would be produced according to the law of comparative advantage.

German economist Friedrich List, on the other hand, saw a different world, a world where a society's success is defined more by what it could produce than by what it consumed. What is good for consumers today is not necessarily what is good for the country long-term: "The forces of production are the tree on which wealth grows. . . . The tree which bears the fruit is of itself of greater value than the fruit itself," List wrote in his seminal work, *The National System of Political Economy*, in 1841. A nation is not measured by its wealth and its purchasing power, but "in the proportion in which it has more developed its powers of production."

National interest, List said, should take precedence over cheap consumer goods purchased from a foreign power. Why, he asked, were European powers able to rule and colonize Asia, Africa, and Latin America? The less-developed countries were not able to make the tools and weapons and machines that they needed. Journalist James Fallows wrote that List argued "that emphasizing consumption would eventually be self-defeating. It would bias the system away from wealth creation—and ultimately make it impossible to consume as much." In List's view, it was not a question of right or wrong, it was simply a question of weak or strong. And he wanted his nation strong.

Other great economic thinkers throughout history have also strongly opposed unrestricted free trade. John Maynard Keynes wrote:

I sympathize with those who would minimize, rather than those who would maximize, economic entanglement between nations. Ideas, knowledge, art, hospitality, travel—these are the things which should of their nature be international. But let goods be homespun whenever it is reasonably and conveniently possible; and above all, let finance be primarily national.

Free trade should never override local customs, laws, environmental protection, and local rights.

As Herman Daly, senior economist with the World Bank, has said, "The domestic economy should be the dog and international trade its tail. GATT seeks to tie all the dogs' tails together so tightly that the international knot would wag the separate national dogs." The real issue is under what set of rules we practice trade: Do we allow unregulated international commerce with no democratic controls? What about the environment? What about worker rights? What protections do we build in for intellectual property rights and how does that interplay with traditional agriculture's communal knowledge? Can we find ways to harmonize upward, so that food safety standards in the United States are not compromised, environmental standards in Germany are not weakened, and health and safety standards in Canada remain strong?

At the very least, even mainstream economists—almost all free traders—are calling for a more lively and vigorous debate about the role of governments in setting rules for corporate behavior in this new era of global capitalism. Fearing the "disproportionate clout on national legislation" that large companies enjoy, Yale School of Management dean Jeffrey E. Garten observed, "the movement of capital has overwhelmed the ability of national governments to manage their economies. Finding the right balance between markets and the public framework in which they operate is the most important issue of our times."

National interest also mattered a great deal to Adam Smith. Regulation of the invisible hand and direction from the government—especially in the areas of commercial navigation, national security, and military preparedness—were of paramount importance. Smith argued that investment at home produces "more revenue and employment" than investment in foreign trade:

> By preferring the support of domestic to that of foreign investment, [the capitalist] intends only his own security; and by directing that industry in such a manner as its produce may be of the greatest value, he intends only his own gain, and he is in this, as in many other issues, led by an invisible hand to promote an end which was no part of his intention.

Four score and some years later Abraham Lincoln echoed Smith's assertion: "Abandonment of the protective policy by the American Government must result in the increase of both useless labour, and idleness; and so, in proportion must produce want and ruin among our people."

Smith was most opposed to mercantilism; he saw merchants set up large corporate monopolies like the East India Company. He seemed to be a free trader sometimes, an anti–free trader other times. But he was never a mercantilist: "The government of an exclusive company is perhaps the worst of all governments for any country whatever." Journalist Jonathan Schlefer, writing in the March 1998 *Atlantic Monthly,* suggests that 1990s globalization is simply a new mercantilism.

In the last twelve years of his life, Smith, as if to convince history

of his true sentiments, worked as a commissioner of customs in Edin-
burgh, a job which charged him with "obstructing imports into Scot-
land" and enforcing Great Britain's protectionist trade policy, mostly
aimed at the fledgling, new country across the Atlantic. "To expect . . .
that freedom of trade should ever be entirely restored in Great
Britain, is as absurd as to expect that an Oceana or a Utopia should
ever be established in it," he told succeeding generations.

8

A Model for Fair Trade and a Call to Action

The liberty of democracy is not safe if the people tolerate the growth of private power to a point where it becomes stronger than their democratic state itself.

—*Franklin Roosevelt, 1938*

We who oppose free trade have a responsibility.

It is not enough to criticize antidemocratic trade agreements. It is not enough to speak out against the Bush Administration's efforts to shift power from democratic governments to multinational corporations. It is not enough to opposed unregulated global commerce. We must advocate trade agreements that include enforceable labor, environmental, and other public interest provisions in the core text of the agreement. After all, what will establish more fertile ground for democracy—a continuation of top-down employers exploiting thirty-cents-an-hour workers, or empowering workers with labor rights?

We as a nation should start with our own government, our own corporations, and ourselves. No U.S. company should be provided the rights and privileges normally accorded domestic corporations if that firm, for example, uses child labor or slave labor anywhere in the world. No money from the Department of Defense. No tax subsidies from Washington or from local communities. No tax breaks for research and development. No government contracts. No use of the United States military to protect American companies abroad if they do not show a reciprocated national loyalty.

The 1999 United Nations *Human Development Report* recommended the following:

- New rules for the WTO, including anti-monopoly powers to prevent global corporations from dominating industries;
- A global central bank to act as a lender of last resort to strapped countries and to help regulate finance markets;
- A global investment trust to moderate flows of foreign capital in and out of developing countries and to raise development funds by taxing global pollution or short-term investments;
- New rules on global patents that would keep the patent system from blocking the access of Third World countries to development, knowledge, and health care;
- More flexible monetary rules that would enable developing countries to impose capital controls to protect their economies;
- A global code of conduct for multinational corporations, to encourage them to follow the kind of labor and environmental laws that exist in their home countries.

There is today little congressional and public input into what has always been the arcane process of trade negotiations. Trade Promotion Authority itself need not be constructed in such a way that the public and Congress have no way of knowing, no chance of input, and no possibility of changing trade agreements which are presented to Congress for a vote. Congress should parcel out negotiating authority to the executive branch one responsibility or one step at a time so as not to allow appointed U.S. trade negotiators to lock into trade agreements changes in American law that might very well be unacceptable to the American people.

More important than any other policy is to make trade negotiators accountable to Congress and to the American public. Trade negotiators often have different political philosophies and different goals from the Congress. The lack of oversight by Congress, the paucity of information available to the public, and the secrecy of negotiations allow trade negotiators much more leeway than most members of Congress realize. After the congressional passage of Fast Tack in 1988, as we have seen, President Bush's negotiators largely ignored repeated directives from Congress to make core labor standards a condition of access to U.S. markets.

Under recent Fast Track/Trade Promotion Authority legislation, negotiated trade agreements are subject to an up-or-down vote, with no amendments allowed. Congressional input prior to the completion of the agreement and before the final vote is virtually nil. Instead, Congress should be required to vote on the proposed text of the actual agreement before the United States actually signs the agreement. Congress then, with public input, could "fix" an agreement that the American people do not like.

While it is clear that Congress will not repeal the North American Free Trade Agreement, it is important that we learn from the shortcomings in that trade agreement. Public Citizen Global Trade Watch proposed the following:

Snap back emergency tariffs.

Tariffs would go into effect when imports in a defined commercial, service, or industrial sector surge. Given the battering that many U.S. manufacturers, most notably steel, took from 1998–2002, this is an essential component in any trade agreement. The trigger needs to be set, unlike the way it was done in NAFTA, so that such tariffs will really go into effect.

Food safety country of origin labeling, and better inspection procedures.

While U.S. Department of Agriculture inspectors are able to visit foreign meat and poultry farms and processing plants, fruits and vegetables have far fewer protections. A good trade agreement would provide multilateral capability. In addition, we should insist that any pesticides banned in the United States could not be applied to fruits and vegetables grown elsewhere which are going to be imported to the United States.

Goods made here or abroad by anyone under the age of fifteen should be denied access to our market.

Amazingly, a unilateral ban by a country on child labor might be a violation of the World Trade Organization. Article XX[e] prohibits prison labor, but there is apparently no provision allowing a prohibition on the sale or refusal to purchase on the basis of differences in the mode of production.

We should devise tax penalties for companies that relocate to nations that have not signed trade agreements including worker rights, and health and safety provisions.

Countries which don't treat their workers fairly should not be so attractive for foreign investors; the race to the bottom on labor and environmental standards will continue unabated otherwise.

Market access should be contingent on working toward and achieving food safety, environment, labor, and human rights standards.

The term "equivalence," a common term used in trade agreements to undermine health and safety standards, should be explicitly defined to mean "guaranteeing minimally the same level of substantive and procedural safeguards as domestic law."

In Harry Wu's 1996 book *Troublemaker,* human rights activist Jeff Fiedler suggested a solution for Smoot-Hawley forced labor violations: Just inspect all China imports for possible products made in Chinese labor camps. "They could do it in one port, maybe Seattle. Send just two inspectors out there and you'd have ships backed up all the way to Hawaii." It would send a message to Chinese officials and American businessmen, who all too often look the other way.

They had seen a lot. Incredible exploitation of defenseless workers. Unspeakable poverty. Cruelty to children as they worked twelve-hour days, seven-day weeks. Andrew Kailembo, general secretary of the African Region of the International Confederation of Free Trade Unions, lamented to a group of representatives in then-Democratic whip David Bonior's office that the World Bank, with crucial U.S. support, insisted that Uganda drop its labor laws and downgrade its Ministry of Labor in order to qualify for World Bank assistance. As the standard of living for most Ugandans dropped, and because the safety net was in tatters, people suffered. Said Kailembo, "In the West they then call Uganda a success story. What industrial democracies should have to do is compete on fair labor standards; that is they should have to use the labor laws in their country when they do business in Africa."

Western countries say that we should use our value system and point to our prosperity, strong middle class, and political liberty to convince developing nations to do the right thing. But Bill Brent, a British trade unionist who serves as the chair of the Workers' Group of the International Labor Organization, shrugged, "Moral suasion might work in a country where citizens can express themselves at the ballot box. But in other countries—Burma and China, for instance—moral suasion simply doesn't work."

These workers, representing Africans, Asians, South Americans, Europeans, and North Americans, were activists in the International Labor Organization, an umbrella group for most of the world's trade unionists.

In June 1998, in Geneva, the International Labor Organization passed the Declaration on Fundamental Principles and Rights at Work, a document which serves as the blueprint for environmentalists, progressives, human rights activists, and trade unionists around the world when lobbying their governments during trade negotiations: It "declares that all Members . . . have an obligation . . . to respect, to promote and to realize . . . the principles concerning the fundamental rights . . . of . . . (a) freedom of association and the effective recognition of the right to collective bargaining; (b) the elimination of all forms of forced or compulsory labour; (c) the effective abolition of child labour; (d) the elimination of discrimination in respect of employment and occupation."

A Model Trade Agreement

In the United States there is an equally important model. House Concurrent Resolution 295, "The Fair Trade for the Future" resolution which I introduced in November 2005 with bipartisan sponsorship, sets out principles for future trade agreements:

> Enforceable worker protections, modeled on International
>   Labor Organization standards;
> Environmental provisions enforceable on par with commercial

provisions and consistent with Multilateral Environmental Agreements;

Safeguards for independent family farmers and enhancement of global food security;

Investment rules protecting foreign investors from expropriation of their property, with the recognition that public interest laws not be exposed to challenge by foreign investors;

Retention of federal, state, and local governments' ability to use procurement as a policy tool, including Buy America laws and purchasing preferences for small, minority- or women-owned businesses;

Preserving the right of governments to maintain essential public services and to regulate private sector services in the public interest;

Promoting access to affordable, vital medicines.

H Con Res 295 will serve as an organizing tool for outside groups—trade advocacy organizations, organized labor, environmentalist, and human rights advocates—to rally around and to lobby Congress on what we should do on future agreements.

Congress should also consider an international minimum wage, suggested by House Democratic Leader Richard Gephardt: a lower minimum wage in poor countries than ours, but an enforceable floor on wages in the developing world. Columbus activist Ted Schaefer, who calls himself "a concerned American," proposes a higher World Wide Minimum Wage, which would establish what he calls "a global leveling factor." If the stated goals of our trade policy are to create wealth and increase exports for U.S. firms, higher wages in the developing world would be an important step. As workers in Mexico or China or Nicaragua earn higher wages, they can then afford to buy American products.

Improving the North American
Free Trade Agreement

In December 2002 in Cuernavaca, Mexico, a small city one hundred miles south of Mexico City, David Bonior and Carlos Heredia had an idea. Bonior, who was about to leave Congress after twenty-six years, and Heredia, a Mexican economist and former congressman, had opposed NAFTA in 1993 and now, almost a decade later, believed that it was still not working—for either Mexico or for the United States.

NAFTA, they explained, was sold to Congress, and to the people of Mexico and Canada as a narrow, stand-alone trade agreement—no more, no less. It was a 1,000-page blueprint that recognized only one class of citizenship—the multinational corporation. NAFTA's aim was to expand trade, not to integrate the three countries and raise wages, nor strengthen environmental rules and labor standards. It had without doubt boosted North America trade and investment, securing access to the U.S. market for the other two nations.

But NAFTA was solely an "economic constitution." What Mexico, the United States, and Canada needed now, Bonior asserted, was a three-country Bill of Rights. "The convergence of our three nations is fundamentally elitist. What it lacks are citizens."

Certain that Congress would not repeal NAFTA in the foreseeable future, Bonior and Heredia proposed a North American Parliamentary Union (NAPU), modeled roughly on the European Union. Instead of a free flow of capital and goods but nothing more, NAPU would, over time, help increase wages, strengthen labor rights, and upgrade environmental and food safety rules.

The seed for this idea may have been planted in December 1998 in a conversation that Bonior, Berkeley professor Harley Shaiken, and I had with the then largely unknown governor of the Mexican state of Guadalajara. A supporter of NAFTA, and a former CEO of Coca-

Cola/Mexico, Vicente Fox was then a candidate for president of his country. Fox told us, a bit wistfully, that the European Union did it right, and NAFTA did not. Integrating poorer European countries—Portugal, Spain, Ireland, Greece—into the more affluent European Union was done slowly, but in a planned, directed way. The candidate of the conservative party, the PAN, Fox surprised us with his view of the EU and of NAFTA: "Market forces," he told Bonior, "will never, in undeveloped countries, be the guiding positive force we need." The European Union had dedicated one-third of its total budget—$35 billion a year—to narrowing the gap between the least and most affluent nations of Europe. Fox said that our actions come "from intelligence, from human action, and not from the market."

In Europe, member nations had a goal to bring in these countries and assist them in achieving 80 percent of the EU's per capita income. And in only a decade, the EU brought these nations from 50 percent of the EU average in per capita income to an astounding 90 percent. The markets in the four less affluent countries grew significantly, making them much more attractive to other EU countries, and immigration from Portugal, Spain, Ireland, and Greece slackened. Today, the EU elects a parliament with real power, has accepted a single currency, and is focused on raising living standards in the four less affluent nations. And now, since May 1, 2004, the EU is made up of twenty-five countries with 455 million people.

Over the same decade, Mexico had seen much less progress. And the Mexican people were no longer so willing to wait for NAFTA's promised results. In late 2003, Heredia told me that the promises to him and to Mexico sounded so empty. "They told us, 'If you sell off the banks to foreign investors, you will grow.' Then they told us, 'If you enter GATT, you will grow.' Then they told us, 'If you join NAFTA, you will grow.' Now they tell us, 'If you sell off PEMEX [the government oil and chemical company], you will grow.' " Mexicans

had watched their one-party government botch the privatization of
state-controlled banks in the early 1990s, which cost Mexican taxpayers in excess of $100 billion to save the nation's financial system from
collapse, and which resulted in 85 percent of the nation's banking system becoming foreign-owned.

And NAFTA, according to economist Jeff Faux, "is leading the
way straight back to the circa 1890 laissez-faire system: commerce
unfettered by other stakeholders." Half of Mexico's population lives
on less than two dollars a day. And economic growth has remained
unchanged from the decade before NAFTA to the decade since—at a
rather anemic 2.7 percent. NAFTA had failed in large part because it
was never intended to build a civil society in Mexico. "Salinas's greatest error," former Clinton official Arturo Valenzuela told me in December 2003, "was that he thought he could do *perestroika* without
glasnost."

That is the reason that Bonior and Heredia have proposed the
North American Parliamentary Union—initially to serve in an advi-
sory capacity for the three nations' legislative and executive leaders,
but eventually to give it more power and a budget that could bring the
three nations together in a coordinated, integrated way.

Others, such as conservative American economist Gary Hufbauer
and Mexican economist Gustavo Vega-Canovas, have proposed other
ways to integrate our three nations. They suggest a Common Fron-
tier, where the integration of the three countries goes far beyond tariffs and investment and trade. They advocate easing of border
crossings, immigration reform, and even a NAFTA Coast Guard and a
NAFTA intelligence agency.

Instead of widening the economic gap, our goal should be to
bring Mexico to the levels of Canada and the United States, something NAFTA neither intended to do, nor was equipped to do.

The formulation of trade policy by the United States government has failed the American people. It is too closed and too arcane. It results in a rapidly spinning revolving door for our trade negotiators to become trade specialists for private American and international businesses. We should, as Congresswoman Marcy Kaptur (D-Ohio) has proposed, develop a professional trade corps similar to the Foreign Service—perhaps even hire older, more experienced people with extensive backgrounds in negotiating contracts and who have no interest in cashing in on their government service in the private sector, people who would drive hard bargains on behalf of labor and environmental standards.

Several effective approaches for change have worked. While most of these ideas demand some action by governments through trade negotiations or at minimum through legislation, one idea that has begun to take root is a simple one. The Grameen Bank in Bangladesh was created twenty years ago to assist the poorest people with very small loans called microcredits. Microcredits provide economic opportunity to some of the poorest people in the world—from the shantytowns of an African township to the slums of Philadelphia to the delta areas of Bangladesh. Microcredit has worked in Asia, Latin America, Africa, and even in the United States, reaching about eight million microentrepreneurs. The United States Agency for International Development (USAID) has played a significant, but unfortunately declining role. In 1994, USAID invested $137 million in microcredits, but with the overall decline in foreign aid, AID administrators have cut expenditures for microcredits. Tens of millions of families who need just minimal assistance to become self-supportive have no access to credit.

The Bank has lent an average of less than $200 to 2.4 million borrowers in Bangladesh, for small entrepreneurs—95 percent to women—to start family businesses. Amazingly, fully 98 percent of the loans have been repaid in full and on time. This "bottom up" model of economic growth has been copied in every continent on earth. In a sense, it is a drop in the ocean, but with Western help, the credit could be extended to the tens of millions of poor but eager entrepreneurs who need it.

Joanne Carter of RESULTS*—an international volunteer group that has been extraordinarily successful in combating world hunger through microcredits, lobbying Congress for the poor, and educating the public—estimates that one million dollars in loan capital invested in a microcredit program will generate 15 million dollars in small loans and three million in savings in just five years because of high repayment rates. The money is recycled because the 98 percent loan repayment rate is higher than perhaps any commercial bank in the world.

Visit Your Representative

Insist to your representative and senator that any trade agreement includes—in the core of the agreement—enforceable environmental standards and worker rights. Weak, unenforceable language written into side agreements is not acceptable; NAFTA negotiators, to mollify environmental and labor critics, wrote weak standards into side agreements. They have meant next to nothing.

Insist to your representative and senators that the United States, when negotiating trade agreements, require fair recompense for other nations' duty-free access to our markets. The U.S. market is the biggest prize in the economic world. Every country and every export business in the world want access to it. Other nations should pay fairly for the privilege—giving us access to their markets, providing

---

* Half of the author's proceeds from this book go to this organization.

political and economic opportunities for their people, guaranteeing enforceable labor and environmental standards as part of their nation's body of law.

Insist to your representative and senators that we work to raise standards around the world; that we never harmonize health and safety standards downward; that we export the values that we as a nation hold dear: human rights, religious freedom, pure food, clean air and water, worker dignity.

And when visiting your representative or senator, remember a few simple rules. Take a small group of people—perhaps four or five, from an environmental group, or trade union, or consumer organization, or a church, or simply like-minded people who care about social justice in our trade policy. Tell the appointments secretary in the congressional office that you will be bringing several people from your organization. Upon meeting the representative, everyone should introduce herself and tell her affiliation.

Give the congressman or congresswoman personal life experience, if possible, illustrating why our trade policy is wrongheaded. Involve everyone in the group; each should say something. Be brief. Don't read from a fact sheet. Keep it as personal and substantive as possible.

Leave a short, one-page fact sheet with the legislator. Each person who attends the meeting should follow up with a short, personal note—handwritten or otherwise—to the representative. Feel free to write to your senator and congressman regularly, whenever trade legislation comes before the Congress, and reference the meeting that you attended.

9

The Battle over the Central American Free Trade Agreement

If they had voted their conscience, CAFTA would have failed by fifty votes in the House.

—*Augustine Tantillo,*
American Manufacturing Trade Action Coalition

The titanic battle over the Central American Free Trade Agreement has forever changed the debate about globalization. On the surface, a trade agreement with six small countries, mostly the poorest nations in our hemisphere, should have little economic or historic significance.

But CAFTA was much more than that. For the first time, labor standards—more precisely, the absence of them—rose to the top of the trade agenda. The American public listened to—and heard—the voices of workers and advocates for the poor in the developing world. Dozens of members of the House and Senate began to see the pain inflicted on American families and communities from wrongheaded trade policy. President Bush submitted the Central American Free Trade Agreement to Congress in May 2004. The arguments had all been heard before: free trade creates jobs in the United States; free trade lifts up workers in the developing world so that they can buy American exports; free trade will bring democracy to authoritarian countries.

But, this time, no one seemed to be listening. President Bush and House Majority Leader Tom DeLay, who wanted to bring CAFTA up for a vote sooner rather than later, postponed the vote until after the election, understanding both its shallow support and its political danger to the Republican Party.

Soon after the new Congress convened and President Bush was inaugurated in January 2005, our CAFTA Whip Meetings began in my office. Initially we met every couple of weeks, and as the vote drew nearer, more frequently. We met in my office—initially only a couple members of Congress, and ten to fifteen staff people representing other congressional offices. We discussed who was with us, who was against us, who was in play. At each whip meeting, we meticulously— one name at a time—analyzed each member in question, determined who best to talk to him or her, figured out what arguments would work best, and then assigned that member to a colleague. As the vote approached, more members of Congress and more staff would come to the whip meetings as we winnowed the undecided members to single digits.

Brett Gibson, who handled trade issues for my office, and Joanna Kuebler, who is our office's communication director and who, along with Brett, played a major role in the CAFTA whip operation and anti-CAFTA strategy, kept assiduous lists of members on a scale of one to five: one—solidly with us (a committed vote against CAFTA); two—leaning our way; three—undecided; four—leaning against us; and five—solidly for CAFTA.

Every two weeks or so, I met with Idaho Republican Butch Otter or North Carolina Republican Walter Jones to discuss Republican votes. We were usually joined by sugar lobbyists and others representing small manufacturers and family farmers and ranchers. Then DeLay said the vote would be held in the first part of the 2005 session of Congress. Again the votes simply were not there. GOP leaders then told the media that the vote would be held before Memorial Day. Again, there was not enough support to bring it up. Then came the threats: the Bush administration told us that our government needed CAFTA to fight the war on terrorism; our economy will be damaged if we don't pass this trade agreement; our trading partners' economies will be devastated without CAFTA. But this time, these myths of free trade fell on much less receptive congressional ears. And these myths were rejected by a public that was way ahead of a Congress in thrall to powerful corporate interest groups.

Free traders in Congress had a difficult time convincing their constituents that these trade agreements were working. They had a difficult time explaining why the trade deficit had jumped from $38 billion in 1992, the year that NAFTA negotiations were mostly completed, to $618 billion in 2004. They had a difficult time explaining why the United States had lost 2 million manufacturing jobs in the last five years. And they had a difficult time explaining why CAFTA would make things better, and that the six CAFTA countries would absorb significant amounts of U.S. exports.

The Dominican Republic and the five Central American countries—Honduras, Costa Rica, Guatemala, El Salvador, and Nicaragua—had a combined economic output equivalent to the city of Cleveland, Ohio. The per capita income of a Guatemalan worker is about $2,800 a year, less than one-twelfth of an average American's. It was hard to believe that North American farmers and ranchers, manufacturers, and small businesses were going to export their products in any significant amounts to Central American countries. Night after night, Democrats and Republicans took to the House floor, outlining the problems with the agreement. CAFTA, New Jersey Democratic Congressman Bill Pascrell said, was not about Central American workers buying apparel from North Carolina or cars manufactured in Detroit or computers from Austin.

Invoking Ben Franklin's "the definition of insanity is doing the same thing over and over and expecting different results," I asked my colleagues on the House floor to refrain from the predictable folly of rubber-stamping another job-killing trade agreement. What CAFTA was about, Maine Democrat Mike Michaud told us, was U.S. companies moving plants to Honduras, outsourcing jobs to El Salvador, and exploiting cheap labor in Guatemala. California Democrat Hilda Solis, probably the only member of Congress of Central American descent—her family is from Nicaragua and Mexico—said she wanted to promote development in the region, but only with an agreement that "will prevent the exporting of U.S. jobs and the exploitation of workers abroad."

Some evenings, in our floor debates, we discussed who opposed and who supported the trade agreement. And we talked about the opposition to CAFTA from the people of Central America and the Dominican Republic. More than 8,000 Guatemalans protested against CAFTA in March 2004. Tens of thousand of workers in El Salvador demanded that their legislature vote down CAFTA. In Costa Rica 30,000 demonstrators took to the streets to voice their opposition to the Central American Free Trade Agreement.

Religious organizations like the Presbyterian Church USA, Lutheran World Relief, and the Council of Churches of Latin America opposed the agreement. Labor organizations representing 13 million American workers and several hundred thousand Central American workers, environmentalists, and consumer groups asked that the agreement be renegotiated and that a new CAFTA with International Labor Organization standards and enforceable food safety and environment provisions be sent to Congress. Small business organizations and family farmer and family rancher groups voiced opposition. And there was a new entrant in our anti-CAFTA coalition: hundreds of small U.S. manufacturers, crippled by unfair trade practices, U.S. tax law, and cutbacks in federal programs for small businesses.

Three years ago, I was speaking to the Summit County Shop Owners Association, a group of mostly family-owned manufacturing firms in greater Akron. Most of them were small companies, employing between twenty-five and one hundred workers, many of them in their forties and fifties, their workers typically earning $20,000–$40,000 a year. During lunch, one owner walked forward and placed a plastic shopping bag full of flyers on the table in front of me. There were perhaps 250 of them: going-out-of-business sales, companies selling off their equipment, companies downsizing. Small manufacturing firms from all over the country, companies with twenty or thirty or forty employees that, when they disappear, the local newspaper hardly takes notice. He told me that he receives this many flyers "every couple of weeks."

These companies—the owners, mostly Republican; the employees, mostly, I would guess, independents and Democrats—knew that trade policy had a lot to do with their demise. They saw their largest customers—the auto companies, large textile companies, other multinational firms—going to China or the Caribbean or Mexico. They knew that their government didn't seem to care much. And many of them were joining us in the fight against CAFTA.

The White House campaign for CAFTA, on the other hand, was always from the top down. United States Trade Representative Rob Portman, formerly an ultra-conservative Republican congressman from Cincinnati, used his office and connections with his former colleagues to lobby personally in the halls of Congress, cutting deals on behalf of the White House.

Thomas Donohue, president and CEO of the U.S. Chamber of Commerce, who had spent extravagantly to push through Trade Promotion Authority 217–216 and then only half-jokingly said he didn't want to buy a landslide, made a much more serious case for CAFTA: "If you are going to vote against CAFTA, it's going to cost you," he warned during a meeting on Capitol Hill of leaders of a 500-plus business-trade association coalition. House members knew he was talking about campaign contributions.

Portman and his USTR predecessor Robert Zoellick had taken care of some of the most powerful interest groups in Washington. Oil interests, Big Tobacco, insurance companies, and the U.S. drug industry had all played prominent roles in President Bush's reelection campaign and had been rewarded handsomely in these trade negotiations. Perhaps the best example was the U.S. pharmaceutical industry's influence on our trade policy. In 2004 the Guatemalan legislature enacted a law allowing the sale of generic drugs to give its citizens more consumer choice and to bring down the price of name-brand drugs. Consumers in Guatemala, the second-poorest country in our hemisphere, cheered them on.

Then the U.S. drug industry and its allies in the Bush administration moved in. Even though international trade law and World Trade Organization rules allow the sale of generics in member countries, the USTR told Guatemalan leaders that there would be no Central American Free Trade Agreement unless the Guatemalan government gave the drug companies what they wanted. Not surprisingly, and against the vociferous opposition of many, the Guatemalan legislature repealed their new public health law. That kind of thing— presidents named Bush teaming up with companies like Pfizer—is nothing new. In 1991 the first President Bush told the Canadians that, unless they repealed their compulsory license law, which ensured significantly lower prescription drug prices for Canadians than Americans were paying, Canada would be excluded from the North American Free Trade Agreement. Ottawa repealed its law, and soon after Canada was included in the NAFTA agreement.

But this time, citizens of the victimized country took to the streets. In mid-March, thousands of demonstrators assembled to protest the inclusion of Guatemala in the flawed Central American Free Trade Agreement. Among their grievances? That CAFTA undercut their democratic rights and sold out their sovereignty. And that patent rules and the action of the Guatemalan legislature would limit the poor's ability to get life-saving medicine. The Bush-pharmaceutical alliance, they maintained, would make a poor country even poorer.

Police used tear gas and water cannons to disperse the crowds after demonstrators hurled rocks and bottles at them. Many were arrested and detained. In one of the demonstrations, two protestors were killed by police and many were injured. Interestingly, but perhaps not surprisingly, inside the U.S. trade representative's office can be found an office for East Asia and the Pharmaceutical Industry, which is charged with looking out for pharmaceutical interests. Harold Meyerson, writing for the pro-CAFTA *Washington Post*, called the USTR a "sales representative for the pharmaceutical industry."

Meyerson—along with Bob Kuttner, David Sirota, Bill Greider, John Nichols, Bob Scheer, Molly Ivins, and Arianna Huffington—was in a distinct minority among the nation's premier writers on trade issues; almost every newspaper editorial board, without seeming to have any doubt, had lined up with the *Wall Street Journal* as cheerleaders for American trade policy for a decade, and none seemed to question their decade of decisions. The largest newspaper in the country to oppose NAFTA in 1993 was the Pulitzer Prize–winning *Toledo Blade,* a gutsy newspaper with a crusading publisher. They recognized what wrongheaded trade agreements had done to their community—to its factories and families, to its police and schools, to its restaurants and small businesses.

Twelve years and literally 4 trillion dollars of trade debt later, we still had no help—and little even-handed coverage—from the corporate-dominated mainstream media. America's newspaper publishers, always in thrall to their largest corporate advertisers, loved this trade agreement as much as they had loved NAFTA and Permanent Normal Trade Relations with China. Editorial writers, like successive birds flying off a power line, rushed their pro-CAFTA editorials into print. Business sections chimed in with plentiful quotes from free-trade cheerleaders and scant mention of opposing arguments. They seemed not to notice that our nation had an exploding trade deficit, our communities were hemorrhaging manufacturing jobs, and our workers were victims of stagnant wages.

But then again, editorial writers and publishers are not particularly threatened by outsourcing or newspaper closings.

Confirming our suspicions about a pro–free trade media bias, Stephen Norton, the main correspondent for the once-respected *Congressional Quarterly,* seemed disdainful of the arguments against the agreement, when he even had time to write our viewpoint. Neither Joanna nor I was surprised when, not too long after the vote, Norton accepted a job with the U.S. trade representative as a speechwriter.

In the weeks leading up to the vote, the presidents of Nicaragua, Honduras, El Salvador, Guatemala, the Dominican Republic, and Costa Rica,went on a tour of the United States sponsored and paid for by the U.S. Chamber of Commerce. They visited Los Angeles, Houston, Cincinnati, and New York, mostly extolling the virtues of unregulated free trade. But there was one problem for the choreographed tour: President Abel Pacheco of Costa Rica announced that he could not support the agreement unless an independent commission found it would not hurt workers in his nation.

CAFTA may have been an agreement with six nations whose combined economy is no larger than that of Cleveland, Ohio. But the public knew that CAFTA mattered—and the American people understood why. Americans intuitively understand that our trade policy has undermined their wages. They understand that our trade policy has cost our community jobs. They understand that plant closings—brought on in large part by corporate trade and tax policies—break up families, erode their communities' tax base, and cause massive layoffs of police, firefighters, and teachers.

Our trade policy encourages American companies to go overseas to seek the lowest labor costs, the weakest environmental laws, the most nonexistent worker protections. Unless workers make concessions . . . major concessions. Lower pay. Less health insurance. Cutbacks in pensions.

Yet American workers know that they are fabulously more productive but have little to show for it. Trade policy, as David Sirota points out, "strips American workers of their leverage to demand better pay." In the last thirty years, the average wage, adjusted for inflation, has increased about 10 percent while worker productivity has jumped about 90 percent. Corporate profits are up. Executive salaries and bonuses have skyrocketed. Yet wages are stagnant.

Since I came to Congress in 1993, trade fights had always taken place in the House. The Senate—where members raised more money from Wall Street, corporate interests, and free-trade ideologues—never seemed to be in play. NAFTA passed 61–38, PNTR for China glided through 83–15, and Trade Promotion Authority was approved 64–34. However, this time, for at least a while, it seemed different.

Democrats Byron Dorgan, Mark Dayton, and John Kerry weighed in. Republicans Larry Craig, Lindsay Graham, and Conrad Burns spoke out. Some joined us for news conferences, others offered amendments in committee.

But, in the end, except for one dramatic moment, most of the action took place in the House of Representatives. During the week of the Senate committee markup of the bill, six legislators from Central America flew to Washington, D.C., to join several of us in the House at an anti-CAFTA news conference. They had planned to also attend the Senate markup, hoping to offer a firsthand perspective on what their constituents had to say about the flawed agreement. They wanted what the bipartisan opposition to CAFTA in the U.S. wanted: to renegotiate.

Joanna Kuebler, the communications director in my office, helped plan their visit and was in the middle of the controversy. Here is how she tells it:

"Standing true to their well-earned reputation for thwarting the democratic process, Republican leadership engaged in a series of stunts that day, knowing that CAFTA opponents would make their way to Capitol Hill. They denied us the right to reserve seats for visiting dignitaries. 'We don't reserve seats,' they told me.

"They moved the hearing from a large room, traditionally used for such a major piece of legislation, to a small meeting room—to limit access. To further dwindle down the number of people the room could hold, they removed seats and placed, in the middle of the room, an enormous conference table roughly twenty feet long that easily took up fifty or more seats.

"Our office had sent interns over to the Senate 'meeting' room at eight A.M. to save seats for the Central American legislators; the hearing was scheduled to start at ten A.M. When the interns arrived just before eight, the line to get in the hearing was around the corner, extending several hundred feet. 'Placeholders' had been hired to stand in line and take up available spots. We'd come to learn that most were paid to hold spots for K Street lobbyists and other CAFTA supporters.

"Six legislators had flown thousands of miles to be heard and found themselves treated by Republican leadership with disrespect and disregard. One thing the Republicans did not count on was the support of Congressman Brown and his entire staff. As soon as we realized what was transpiring, a group of ragtag Democratic press and legislative staff flew into action. I'd like to say we had a well-thought-out strategy for countermeasures.

"In truth, we worked fast, and made it up as we went along. Holding my trusty staff badge and news releases high in hand, I pushed past a Brooks Brothers-clad gatekeeper and made my way to the press box. The senators were going to sit around a gargantuan conference table, while the press took seats on the dais usually saved for elected officials. Remembering the refusal Republican leadership gave us to reserve seats for foreign dignitaries, I was angered when I came across a sea of seats, all of them reserved. I saw signs that said, 'Reserved for Chamber of Commerce,' 'Reserved for USTR,' and so on.

"I clued the press in on what was happening, and passed out copies of the testimony given to me by the Central American legislators. I'd like to say the media was as outraged as were many of us that day. I'd love to be able say they wrote about the miscarriage of justice playing out before their very eyes.

"Out of two dozen reporters from around the world present that day, not one wrote about the Republican tactics. Or the Central American legislators. Or their testimony. I was about to head out of the room when the doors were opened to the public and the traffic began to flow in, past the gatekeeper who checked each name on his clipboard before letting people pass. Working on sheer adrenaline (and really, not much forethought at all), I called out for a fellow press secretary standing in the hallway to run and grab the legislators (who were in line about a quarter of a mile away). To this day, I'm not sure how it happened—I remember seeing a legislator nearing the doorway, reaching past the gatekeeper, grabbing her hand, and telling her colleagues to follow me. I didn't think the Republicans would go so far as to create an international incident in front of the global press.

"The seven of us rushed past the gatekeeper—who was at once confused and outraged—clearly he had not counted on our scrappy resolve and sheer determination. I found the legislators seats in the corner of the room and told them in my very broken Spanish to 'just sit. Stay seated. Don't move.'

"They sat down, I ran out of the room—they got to stay. They did not get to be heard that day. They had to bear silent witness to the markup of a bill they knew would hurt their constituents. And yet they stayed to the very end of the day, determined that they would not be turned out. Just their presence in that room was a huge success for them—for us all—given the forces we were up against.

"That's what it takes to get access to the democratic process around here these days."

In the end, CAFTA passed the Senate by a much smaller margin than other trade agreements, 55–45, setting up a showdown in the House.

Even though CAFTA passed the Senate by the smallest margin ever for a trade agreement and House Republicans knew that they were losing with the public, GOP leadership in the House of Representatives rolled the dice. Among other things, GOP leadership rescheduled the vote on the pork-laden-something-for-everyone highway bill, delaying it until the day after the CAFTA vote and reminding members that they were watching their vote on the controversial trade agreement. Then-Majority Leader Tom DeLay brought up CAFTA late on a Wednesday night in July 2005. Earlier in the day, President Bush made a rare visit to huddle with Republicans for ninety minutes at the weekly closed-door meeting of the Republican Conference, telling them—what else?—that he needed CAFTA for the war on terrorism. Vice President Cheney, who has appeared in public and talked to the press more infrequently than any vice president in memory, spent much of the day in the Capitol. As the vote approached, Republican member after Republican member was ushered into a room no more than fifty feet from the House floor to be persuaded by the vice president.

Earlier in the evening, I appeared with Arizona Republican Jim Kolbe to discuss the impending vote; Kolbe had told a reporter, in light of reports that CAFTA would come up short, that "arms would be twisted into a thousand pieces." We knew that we had won on the merits; we had proposed a trade agreement that reflected the growing call for change in U.S. trade policy, one that included strong worker and environmental standards, one that would respect American businesses and workers and lift up living standards in Central America.

As the leader of the anti-CAFTA whip operation, I knew that we had promises of 187 or 188 votes from Democrats, and 30 to 32 votes from Republicans; several other Republicans told my friend Walter Jones (R-NC) and outside groups that they were leaning our way. That exceeded the 217 votes (there was one vacancy in Congress) that we needed to win. Once the vote was called at about 11:05 P.M., it looked like a Bush cabinet meeting was in progress in the hall outside the House chamber. It seemed that secretaries of every department were talking to reluctant GOP members. Republican members told the *Washington Post* that many of the favors bestowed in exchange for their votes would be tucked into the huge energy and highway bills that Congress was scheduled to pass the next day. Or favors withheld.

Democratic leader Nancy Pelosi said that the activity outside the House chamber "looked like an episode of *Let's Make a Deal*." Others said it resembled the wheeling and dealing on a car lot.

One Republican told me the next day that, in order to avoid the arm-twisting, he voted as soon as the vote was called, jumped in his car, and "was across the Fourteenth Street bridge headed home before any of my leadership knew I was gone."

After about thirty minutes—votes are usually final in about eighteen or nineteen minutes—opponents were leading. Ten minutes later, supporters of CAFTA had pulled ahead by three votes, 214–211. Nine members—all Republicans, all publicly committed to their constituents or the media, or privately to their colleagues to vote no on the agreement—had yet to vote; they apparently had promised DeLay that they would wait before casting their votes against CAFTA. DeLay knew that he would need some of them, and that the rest of them could be given a pass; they all were willing to cooperate with him. Five of those nine had publicly promised—through news conferences or speeches—that they were voting no. The others had told labor or business groups that they could be counted on to oppose the trade pact.

Then Patrick McHenry, a North Carolina Republican, voted no. Then Robin Hays, another North Carolina Republican, and the same man—amazingly—who had changed his vote to pass Trade Promotion Authority four years ago by one vote, switched his vote from no to yes.

Mike Fitzgerald (R-Pennsylvania) voted yes, followed by Steven LaTourette (R-Ohio). That let off the hook Bobby Jindal (R-Louisiana), Charles Boustany (R-Louisiana), Robert Simmons (R-Connecticut), Shelley Capito (R-West Virginia)—all of whom were "released by Republican leadership" to vote no, and all of whom were facing difficult reelection contests. Two representatives who had promised to vote no left the floor and did not vote: Jo Ann Davis (R-Virginia) and Charles Taylor (R-North Carolina). At 12:09 A.M. on Thursday morning, after a vote of more than an hour, the Speaker gaveled that the Central American Free Trade Agreement had passed: 217–215. In essence, by one vote. If one person had switch his vote, it would have tied and therefore been defeated. In case there was anyone left in our country who actually believed that newspaper editorial boards really cared about good government and the public interest, LaTourette's hometown newspaper lauded his middle-of-the-night conversion, saying he did the right thing.

In early September, the U.S. Chamber of Commerce kept its word: it sponsored a large fund-raising event, and then its members did a series of smaller fund-raising events thanking the CAFTA 15, the lone Democrats who voted for the agreement. "The word went out, no doubt about it," a lobbyist told *The Hill* newspaper, "that now is the time to show the love." Another lobbyist chimed in, "The issue was really important to us. We wanted to show them how much we appreciated that they walked the plank on it." The Chamber of Commerce especially rallied around freshman conservative Democrat Henry Cuellar, holding two fund-raisers for him in south Texas and one in Washington.

At a celebration at a more downscale restaurant with Representative Walter Jones, more than a dozen other House members, and more than a hundred people from our religious-labor-human rights-business-agriculture coalition opposing CAFTA, we believed that we did indeed have something to celebrate.

All elements of the Democratic caucus—the Congressional Black Caucus and the blue dogs, the progressives and the New Democrats, the Congressional Hispanic Caucus and those who belong to no faction—are now in general agreement on trade. Fully 93 percent of House Democrats had opposed CAFTA. Comparable numbers would vote for a strong trade agreement that incorporates International Labor Organization standards, human rights, and food safety and environmental protections. And there is substantial support among Republicans for a trade agreement with labor and environmental standards. Walter Jones, the conservative and deeply religious man from North Carolina, led the Republican whip against CAFTA by appealing to religious principles, family values, and a "we're-all-in-this-together" philosophy. Democrats and Republicans of faith—whether a faith in God or a faith in our country to live up to the promise of America—have found common ground on our trade policy. The only way that the free-trade fundamentalists could win was to literally buy the deal, in the middle of the night, under the cover of darkness. And although we lost the congressional vote in the black of night, we knew that we had won the public debate in the light of day.

Several months later, on a cold December day in Steubenville, an industrial city on the Ohio River, Congressman Ted Strickland, the Democratic candidate for governor of Ohio, told 200 political activists, "Six months ago, there was no one in the United States Senate like Sherrod Brown who was organizing, speaking out, buttonholing his colleagues, building the case against CAFTA. If Sherrod Brown had been a member of the Senate last summer, CAFTA would not be the law of the land." I didn't know if he was right, but I was convinced that the Senate was our best chance to change trade policy. The narrow defeat of CAFTA in the House—clearly a result of backroom deals, sleazy politics, and House rules that can accomplish for the majority party anything that its unprincipled leaders want—made me begin to reexamine a job I love. It was becoming clear to me that the House deck was stacked. And it was becoming more clear that U.S. trade policy—at the margins and in total—could be challenged and redirected in the Senate.

The dog days of summer after the CAFTA vote gave me and Connie time to look at our lives together. We moved to Avon, a small community east of Lorain. By September, family issues began to be resolved. Our oldest daughter Emily married Mike Stanley, a young man from Baltimore whom we love; Andy was getting his PhD at Ohio State; Elizabeth was returning to college; and Caitlin was about to start college. After lengthy discussions with our children, Connie and I made the decision. I would enter the race for the United States Senate.

Just as importantly, we decided that the race for the U.S. Senate, in perhaps the most important swing state in the country, would be on my terms. We would run a progressive campaign meant to build a movement around the principles that we hold dear, a campaign to give hope to people who had given up. It would be about issues. It would be a race about the minimum wage and the working poor. It would be about middle-class Ohioans, lost pensions, and U.S. trade policy. It would be about the environment and health care, social justice and patriotism.

We would force reporters to talk about the minimum-wage initiative, a ballot issue that would be a centerpiece of our campaign. We would force reporters to cover the Medicare disaster, a law forced through Congress in the dead of night to feed their drug company and insurance company contributors. We would force reporters to detail the betrayal of American workers by their government and their employers. We would force reporters to cover the Iraq war, to discuss presidential duplicity and explore the distraction of the war-profiteering presidential adviser Karl Rove.

During my announcement tour—a swing through thirteen cities in four days in early December 2005—I saw the hopes and heard the dreams of literally hundreds of Ohioans: from my adopted hometown Lorain to my high school in Mansfield, from a Fair Trade coffeehouse in Toledo to Reverend Fred Shuttleworth's church in

Cincinnati. Their belief in change and their hope for our future told me that a race for the Senate would embolden them to believe they still matter in this country.

Connie and I saw an excitement and a hope in the faces of Ohioans in every part of Ohio that our state and our country could be a better place.

No matter what the outcome on November 7, I knew that we had already won.

No country is as well-situated as the United States to use our economic power to influence economic and non-economic events around the world. We have used our economic leverage to pressure other nations to accept the Washington Consensus. We have exported our accounting rules and our intellectual property rights. We have demanded deregulation of financial markets and privatization of public services. We have even, in some cases, forced the surrender of sovereignty to the interests of multinational investors. As the world's wealthiest nation, with the most lucrative and most attractive market, we should use the unique historical opportunity that now presents itself to also promote freedom and empowerment for workers, the poor, and the middle class throughout the world. As David Sirota writes, there should be a "price of admission" to our marketplace: countries must have enforceable labor standards, human rights, and environment standards if they want to get in.

In the two or three decades after World War II, most trade conducted by U.S. companies was with industrialized countries with political and economic systems similar to our own. Trade negotiations were simpler, more straightforward, and concerned themselves mostly with tariffs and tariff-related issues. Trade discussions centered on lowering tariffs and non-tariff barriers to gain access to each other's markets. Today all that has changed. Our trading partners are often poor, less developed countries, usually with political systems alien to ours.

For the first time in postwar America, more than half our imports come from developing nations, most of them with repressive, autocratic governments that shun political and economic freedoms: from the *maquiladoras* in Mexico, where the plant managers have in essence formed their own guild to determine wages and keep union activity out, to China, where the Communist Party brooks no dissent and allows no discussion about wages, to Indonesia where a corrupt military dictatorship has worked hand in hand with Western companies to keep wages low and workers docile. Together, those three countries represent more than $250 billion in U.S. trade deficits.

If we do not insist on and hold out for labor rights and health and environmental standards in every trade negotiation in which we participate, we will have failed the world and ourselves. If workers at the bottom—children in Indonesian sweatshops, political prisoners in Chinese labor camps, and young, struggling families in Mexico's mills of gold—cannot win the right to organize and bargain collectively for livable wages, safer workplaces, and economic and political freedoms, then wages and living standards in rich and poor nations alike will continue to be pulled downward. The future of the developing world is directly tied to the future of trade unions. Only indigenous trade unions—assisted by the West to be sure, but controlled in each country by local workers—can force Western investors and domestic employers to pay a living wage. Only free-trade unions with the legal power to bargain collectively can force multinational employers to share the wealth that the workers create for their companies. Trade unions at their best utilize the democratic process at work; they allow workers a share of productivity growth brought on by collective bargaining; they give workers the tools to address income inequality.

That is what labor unions did in the West. That is why labor standards are essential in every trade agreement into which we enter.

The United States, with our market of gold and our enormous economic clout, is in a unique position to help empower poor workers in developing countries. When the world's poorest people can buy American products rather than just make them, then we will know that our trade policies are finally working.

Index